A Limited Partnership

A Limited Partnership

THE POLITICS OF RELIGION,
WELFARE, AND SOCIAL SERVICE

Bob Wineburg

Columbia University Press   New York

Columbia University Press

Publishers Since 1893

New York   Chichester, West Sussex

Library of Congress Cataloging-in-Publication Data

Wineburg, Robert J.

A limited partnership : the politics of religion, welfare,

and social service / Bob Wineburg

p. cm

Includes bibliographical references and index

ISBN 0–231–12084–2 (cl—acid free-paper)

ISBN 0–231–12085–0 (pa—acid free-paper)

1. Church charities—United States

2. Social service—United States

HV530.W56   2001

361.7/5 21   00064507

Printed in the United States of America

Designed by Audrey Smith

c 10 9 8 7 6 5 4 3 2 1

p 10 9 8 7 6 5 4 3 2 1

*In rememberance of my deceased parents
and brother Ben, Ruth, and Mike Wineburg
and to the memory of Professor Roy Lubove.*

The spirit of each of them is in this book.

B.

CONTENTS

ACKNOWLEDGMENTS

There are a slew of people that I would like to thank for making this work possible. First is Cate, my wife and partner for the last twenty-seven years. She started Project Independence at Greensboro Urban Ministry in 1984, one of the longest running mentoring programs I know of that tries to match women on welfare, or trying to stay off it, with church members who want to help. Without Cate, I never would have started this line of inquiry with so much attention on the religious community. Right next to her are my kids Zach and Hannah who kept me grounded during my research and writing. If I didn't attend a soccer game, a basketball game, or a play, I would have spent every waking moment on this book. That would not have been healthy.

Of course there is the staff at Greensboro Urban Ministry who, from time to time helped me with questions—Mike Aiken, Nathan Witherspoon, Anne Morelli, and Evelyn Parks always would answer a question when needed. I want to thank Major Tom Jones of The Salvation Army National Headquarters for a great interview, his warmth, and friendship. Thanks to Mike Brogioli and Brian Siebenlist of Catholic Charities USA for their interview, and for keeping me on the AdvoFax. Thanks to Tobi Printz, Tom Pollack, Carol De Vita of The Urban Institute in Washington. Micheline Malson, Kathy Putnam and especially Barbara Earls from the Jubilee Project of The NC Council of Churches kept me updated from the field daily for over 2 years with e-mail and phone calls. Joe Mann of the Duke Endowment was so receptive to the Jubilee Project and deserves a word of thanks too. My great friend Ram Cnaan from Penn's School of Social Work kept me busy during this time with his important findings as did Bob Jaeger and Diane Cohen from Partners for Sacred Places. Bob Williams of Guilford college was awesome in keeping me grounded in my analysis. I take pity on his students. Dr. James Wind President of the Albin Institute gave me my start when he was program officer in the Religion Division of the Lilly Endowment. To you folks I say thanks too.

Bobby Webb the secretary at the Department of Social Work deserves a hug for all of her support, as do the faculty in the Social Work Department for being nice to me, even behind my back. Provost Ed Uprichard and Dean Brad Bartel supported my research leave to get this work finished, and to them I say thanks. Debbie Otis, Carol Sanders and Alana Neal of UNCG's Grants and Contract Office were alawys so helpful—thanks! Reverend Odell Cleveland, Nancy Mclean, Yolanda Baker and Mary Reaves of The Welfare Reform Liaison Project and Pastor George Brooks of Mt Zion Baptist Church kept me involved in the daily life of a real welfare reform effort emerging from a local church. Nathan Cook was a huge part of the story there too. Rob Mc Andrews from Salem State University School of Social Work is the smartest person I know in Social Welfare and Community Practice outside of Ellen Netting of Virginia Commonwealth University. Diana Garland is the mother of Church Social Work and gave me great help when I first got serious about this project. Mark Constantine saved my life in his brief stay in Greensboro because he knows so much about religion and nonprofits. To all of you helpful people, I also say thanks. Sister Jeanne Knoerle SP and Dr.Craig Dykstra of The Lilly Endowment are owed thanks for supporting this work in their own way. Peter Dobkin Hall of Harvard University and Lisa Berlinger the Director of Yale Divinity School's Program on Non Profit Organization, were instrumental in getting this book published here and have been great supporters of my work. To them I also say thanks. Fasih Ahmed, Bridgette McLain, and Mark Sills know I'd still be on page one without them. Jon Van Til gave me a chance early on when no one else thought my early work was important.

The last person I would like to thank on the scholarship side of things, is Debbi Seabrooke, my editor. She can take a diamond in the rough and make it glisten like a star. She was firm but gentle in her criticisms. I thought I could write well, but Debbie did some amazing things with words that sounded good, apparently to just me. I asked her husband Charlie if I could marry her, and he said no! She will continue to be my editor though. Thanks Debbie! My great friends Richie Zweigenhaft, Lisa Young, Kurt Lauenstein, Sherry Dickstein, Svi and Sherry Shapiro supported me in essential ways throughout this process. John Rife, chair of my department, is the best and most supportive boss on the planet. Thanks to Rabbi Fred and Nancy Guttman. I belong to a congregation whose spirit and deeds are internal and communal. That is energizing. Finally, I say thanks to my brother Sam who could have invented the word loyalty. He is always there.

A Limited Partnership

Introduction

In this introduction I start to examine the ideas that gave rise to the current welfare policy in a way that I follow throughout the book. It is a method of analysis that varies from many analyses of social policy because I proceed with one eye glued on the policy debate itself, and the other focused on how the actual implementation of policy affects the delivery of local social services. This way of looking at things adds some new thinking to a central, but untested, idea buoying the 1996 welfare reform legislation. It is the idea that religious congregations and faith-based nonprofit organizations are much better at delivering social services locally than the welfare bureaucracy.

The 1996 legislation not only ended welfare as we knew it, but it also sent the design and delivery of welfare services to states and localities with an assumption that the religious community would be a key player in local welfare efforts. Attached to the legislation was an important stimulus designed to create more religious involvement in local social service delivery. The provision, called Charitable Choice, allows public money to go to religious congregations and faith-based organizations to provide public social services. The details of Charitable Choice are less important at this point in the discussion than its spirit, which is *that the religious community can, should, and is capable of being central* to local welfare efforts. At the heart of the analysis in this book is the effort to bring clarity, specificity, and a deeper understanding of that spirit.

I look carefully throughout the book at the merits of the idea that the religious community is capable of effectively meeting the elaborate needs of poor women who become employed or underemployed when government assistance ends. I show the evolution of the thinking during the last twenty years that got us to the point that politicians of both stripes sincerely, but with little evidence, believe in the capability of religiously based social services to be center stage in welfare provisions. At the same time that I show the development of the thinking that shaped the policy, I give a ground level picture of what the growing collaboration in the local service delivery between the religious and secular systems of service looked like. After examining the new and expanded roles that religious congregations and faith-based nonprofit organizations increasingly assumed locally in the last two decades, I feel safe in arguing, as I do throughout, that the religious community can play an important part in local service provisions, but the expectations put on them are out of proportion to what they can actually deliver.

I have worked closely with, and studied carefully, the agencies and organizations in my community, Greensboro North Carolina. I have seen the interconnections develop among the public agencies, private and faith-based nonprofit organizations, and religious congregations since the budget cuts of the Reagan era. Increasingly it has become apparent to me that the policymaking and the policy delivery system are two very different worlds because there is a substantial gap between what policymakers want to accomplish and what actually happens when their policies get implemented locally. If policymakers could somehow know more about operation the local system of services when they conceptualize their schemes, policies would probably work much better. I try throughout this book to bridge the gap in that understanding.

Welfare policy in this country has always been contentious and complicated enough that practical concerns, such as how a particular policy will actually work locally when implemented, are often buried hot ashes of the policy debate. For example, the current welfare debate is an old, complex, and often antagonistic argument about the nature of human need and how society should respond to those seeking help. Central to this debate is what benefits is one entitled to and what must she do for herself (I use she because welfare policy is aimed at women.) Is she solely responsible for her lot in life as some policymakers contend? Or, do circumstances beyond her control, as others would argue, stop her from mastering her own fate? Where do her children come into play in this crossfire? The system of services in any community is the vehicle through which help is given and received. Its agencies and programs reflect the evolution of national, state, and community policy, and like a kaleidoscope, embody many shapes and dimensions of the dominate and recessive views as they took form locally.

Because over time there has often been a disconnect between the intention of this or that policy and the system and people that carry it out, local delivery systems are not as well oiled and maneuverable as they could have been had their advocates participated in shaping policy. Such an idea on the grand scale is easier said than done. In a nutshell, it means that service providers would have to be able to assess their systems' capabilities, share information with people who lead supporting systems, measure their combined successes, dissect their failures, re-engineer their systems, teamup with policymakers, and redesign policies. There is a chance for this kind of process to work as services devolve to the local level, but the political stakes are too high in contentious policy debates to make practical concerns like "workability" central to the policy argument.

The local system of services is an imprint of the past efforts and a snapshot of present attempts to respond to ever changing needs. The picture is one of an array agencies and programs. They rest on a foundation of ad hoc self-help, organized voluntary responses, and collective or governmental responses—and these are the ones often under attack in this era. The religious community, with its congregations and faith-based nonprofit organizations, sits firmly in the self-help and voluntary mix. But it would be a mistake to assume that the social services provided by the religious community and those provided by the broader locality's public agencies, secular private nonprofit organizations, unincorporated self-help groups, and for-profit social services contractors are not braided. Chapter 4 demonstrates just how intricate these relationships are and shows just how the religious community actually supports the effort of the others. So, a major consequence of a shift in effort by one quarter, (in this case of this book, governmental social welfare policies and programs), forces a shift in others.

Local systems of service over the last sixty years have been twisted and turned to a large extent by changes in national social policy. At particular times, it is fairly easy to determine which point of view about the nature of need dominates and which perspective is subsidiary. Franklin Roosevelt's New Deal polices and programs, and Lyndon Johnson's Great Society policies and programs reflected a framework that made one's *circumstance* the primary cause of need. Governmental intervention, as the thinking in that camp went, changes circumstances more effectively than individual and voluntary responses. The predominate system of private charity gave way to public entitlements. The current discussion about social security reflects a framework of government intervention that changes the *circumstances* of our elderly through basic, but nonetheless permanent, financial and medical support.

President Ronald Reagan's policy of budget cuts and consolidation of federal programs in the early 1980s, President Bush's continued consolidation and focus on individual and voluntary responses by way of his "Points of Light" campaign in the late 1980s and early 1990s, and President Clinton's Welfare Reform of the late 1990s, reflect the view that, in the end, says the *individual* controls her fate. Government policies, starting with President Reagan, began to strongly emphasize the need to reduce government efforts and increase self-help, voluntary, religiously based, and locally designed and delivered efforts. When the New Deal and Great Society programs took over as the predominate providers locally, the other systems of care, secular nonprofit agencies, self-help, and religiously based social services did not vanish from the local scene. They became integral but subsidiary. When the Reagan budget cuts of the 1980s took effect, government programs did not go away either. They changed, as did the other services, especially those emerging from religious congregations and faith-based nonprofit organizations.

The central focus of this book is about the system of service and the role religious congregations and faith-based organizations play in that system. Policymakers and experts often get bogged down in their arguments about which view is right or wrong with little understanding of how a policy change really impacts the local system of services. When one or the other perspective prevails, policy moves from theory to implementation. More often than not, *little or nothing* is done to prepare the people who administer the agencies and programs and serve those in need locally for climatic changes that happen when policy shifts happen abruptly. At present programs are being sent from the federal government to the states and then are implemented at the local level based on the view that the individual and corresponding voluntary and religiously based set of services are the best vehicles to handle the problem of welfare and poverty. This is Devolution.

My thesis has four dimensions. First, I want to emphasize that local social services systems just don't have the capability to handle the complex set of social problems without thoughtful planning. The religious system, where great emphasis has been focused lately, is not set up to take on the role it is being asked to assume. Second, I call for construction of new *partnerships*, and continued support of existing ones, at the local level. Enhancing the system that delivers services will go a long way in clearly defining which providers in the local mix of services can best address the needs that underlie welfare and at what level of provision which provider can be most effective.

My third focus, which sets a tone heard throughout this book, is directed at policymakers. They will be essential in making the indigenous system of services effective in bringing about well-being for people in need. It will be important for them to understand the difference between the rhetoric behind the calls for changing welfare and the reality facing the system of services, and how that system actually operates. Locally, Republican and Democrats, people of all shades of color, and people of all religious persuasions will have to solve complex problems together. While rhetoric and ideology have a place in debate and discussion, they are not replacements for clear-cut problem-solving efforts that have to be done cooperatively at the local level.

So I call for a refrain from grand sweeping and unsupported generalizations about the character of welfare recipients and the nature of public agencies, and instead, call for increased community education about the nature and scope of the intertwined causes of poverty and the system of services and the people involved in trying to ameliorate the problems locally. In chapter 7, I provide a framework to stimulate that understanding. I note in chapter 8 that the religious community may be able to set the moral tone and underlying spirit of cooperation for such discussions.

Fourth, I call on the higher educational establishment to assist their local communities through the collection and analysis of base line information that can help decision makers solve, mange, and prevent unnecessary problems. In chapter 2, I provide ten recommendations for consideration. The rest of the book is a sequential presentation of case material and survey research starting with the budget cuts of the Reagan presidency in 1980. Chapters 1 through 3 focus mainly on the connection between the budget cutting policies of the 1980s and Greensboro's religious and secular responses. Chapter 2 explains why the interconnected domains of policy, religion, and social services were unexamined by scholars. Chapter 4 substantiates an underlying theme of the book—the complex and longstanding relationship between the religious community and the public and private social service system.

Chapters 5 and 6 support and broaden that theme by demonstrating that social service activities of congregations, in collaboration with the community, move congregations from isolated alms-giving to collaborative policy-making. Chapter 7 is a step back in that it provides a detailed examination of how the social service system operates. There is a presentation of two frameworks to understand the intertwined relationships among the partners of secular and sectarian agencies and organizations who deliver services locally. This provides the context for my summoning policymakers and community leaders to develop strong partnerships in local service development. Chapter 8 is a case snapshot of what I think will become commonplace as welfare services become even more local. Chapter 9 presents one statewide and two local religious responses to the new welfare reform and lists responses from around the nation. In the Conclusion I lay out some recommendations that will help policymakers, funders, practitioners, and community leaders start to build better local service systems that strengthen prevailing partnerships.

MY ARGUMENT

Much of what I will argue in this book is based on the idea that the religious community is unable to take over the bulk of governmental social services although both the religious and political right argue that they can and should. I have reached this conclusion after carefully examining how the religious community in Greensboro, North Carolina first responded to the Reagan era budget cuts in public programs in the 1980s and early 1990s, and has been responding to the welfare polices of the Clinton and Gingrich era.

Those policies have culminated in sending welfare responsibilities back to the states and localities. Some might argue that I should not be able to draw general conclusions about social policy, social service, and religion based on an analysis of one community. As it turns out, Greensboro is more or less representative of other communities nationwide and I demonstrate this point throughout this book with case examples from other communities whose experiences are parallel to Greensboro. An important undercurrent throughout is that the religious community can and should be an important partner in service provision locally with public and private nonprofit agencies, no more and no less. Unlike the bulk of policy arguments about the role of religion in the welfare state, my argument is supported by survey research and case evidence. I would like to see more policy discussion about welfare reform, religion, and voluntary and public social services to be less blinded by ideology and more grounded in reality and understanding. This work is a start.

Mine is a practical argument. The Reagan era budget cuts in human services, followed by the new welfare reform in the late 1990s with its focus on local service development, have headed us toward making services completely voluntary and local. This may sound good but the system of services is far too huge and complicated for any one policy to work if wholesale changes come without a well-orchestrated planning and coordination effort. The new shift will cause more confusion to localities than the good it is supposed to do. Someday we might be able to serve those in need without the help of federal, state, or even local government involvement. But for now, more people in state and local governmental agencies, religious congregations and charities, and voluntary agencies are scurrying about trying to plan for something they know very little about and really did not participate in shaping.

Social service systems, and the social problems they are supposed to manage, are far more complex than policy theorists and political pundits imagine, especially when they design the programs that lead the public to believe that all federal involvement is gone. Even with all the talk of ending welfare as we know it, there is still a huge array of federal programs and services still wrapped around local communities and the lives of citizens. They have their unique requirements and procedures. Some are rooted in statute; some are grant-driven. They are often operated by, or work in tandem with states and localities. States and localities in turn are guided by their own intricate laws and well-meaning programs and services, which in turn are steered by polices and procedures designed to ensure an honest measure of success and accountability. The local nongovernmental agencies and programs, like those of the United Way Agencies, constitute one set of tributaries that flow into and out of such a system. Religious congregations, religious charities, and self-help groups constitute another set of tributaries that feed the system of social provisions in a community. For example, our public health system deals with clean water, restaurant cleanliness, and child immunizations, while the United Way's Red Cross agencies collect blood, and often do so at a place of worship. Each entity, public or private, religious or secular, plays a part in ensuring social stability and general public health.

Consequently, it is my contention that local social services systems just don't have the capability to handle the complex set of social problems that come with poverty by arbitrarily reassigning the management of those problems to private local services. The system does not work that way, and the private system of services, especially the religious system, is not set up to take on the role it is being asked to assume.

The new welfare reform policy that went into effect in 1996 is important especially for religious congregations and charities. If a woman does not succeed in the workplace, there is no longer a federal guarantee that financial help will be available. She will have to find support at the local level, and as history has shown us, when all else fails, people rely on their religious community for help. The politicians who designed this new policy had the religious backup system in mind when they voted to shift the welfare programs back to the states and localities. The one thing that they did not quite understand was that the religious community has been intricately involved in social service development and delivery from the beginning of nationhood. The religious community expanded its efforts so much so in the Reagan era that anyone with an understanding of how the network of religious social services operates at the community level knows that in addition it cannot now handle vast numbers of women seeking services to support them while they make the transition from welfare to work. The religious community is not equipped to provide supportive services like transportation, child care, and job training, and beefing itself up to do so on any massive scale is not plausible.

How did we get to a point where politicians could be so blind about the huge increase in service efforts of the religious community in the 1980s and 1990s, while innocently calling on churches and sectarian charities to become the true safety net for the poor as we move into the twenty-first century? I will try to answer that question in the following pages. For now it is important to know that the people who make up the political and religious forces of the right have not been the same people who, since the 1980s, have been delivering the food, providing the shelter, donating the money, and offering an array of other services to local people. People who make up the religious and politically conservative right have been much more involved in shaping a *social agenda* than delivering social services.

This book centers on the thinking that underlies the bitter debates about how to handle social problems effectively, which at the extreme calls for the reassignment of all welfare programs to the church. This is dangerous. It sounds good but it cannot work. To understand the thinking that got us here, it is essential to understand the influence of two conservative thinkers in the 1980s, who, with their artistic and forceful framing of the policy debate, had a gradual but profound impact on how the public would view and talk about welfare concerns. George Gilder and Charles Murray, with the backing of conservative think tanks and foundations, produced works that would influence the national welfare policy debate for years. Gilder's *Wealth and Poverty* (1981) and Murray's *Losing Ground* (1984 [1983]) represented conservative scholarly attempts in the Reagan years to change the discussion about the causes and cures of poverty, from the liberal notions about flaws in the economic system that left the poor on the fringes, to defects in the behavior of the poor and the programs of big government that kept the poor from functioning properly in society. In Gilder's classic 1981 *Playboy* interview, that point is demonstrated. We see how the conservative ideas about the poor start to become part of the public discourse, and we see also Gilder's attack on the liberal perspective of social welfare which I will discuss more fully in a moment.

> **Playboy:** Why do so many well-intentioned government programs wind up achieving precisely the opposite of their planned results?
> **Gilder:** This is the phenomenon that I call moral hazards of liberalism. Moral hazards is an insurance term. It refers to the potentially negative results of an insurance policy. The moral hazard

of fire insurance is arson. When the insurance on a building exceeds its value, spontaneous combustion often results. There's nothing the insurance company can do about it except to reduce the payoff.

Playboy: How does that relate to public policy?

Gilder: The moral hazard of unemployment insurance is unemployment. When government-paid unemployment benefits plus leisure time become greater than the benefits of work, unemployment increases. The moral hazard of welfare tends to be broken families and increased poverty because, when welfare benefits become greater than the benefits of maintaining an intact family with an employed breadwinner, then more and more families will tend to break up and the breadwinner will go to the streets into crime and the underground economy.

With a slightly different twist, Murray (1984), argued that the social programs emerging from the wisdom (he really meant lack of wisdom) of the 1960s, and designed to help welfare families were a failure on pragmatic and moral grounds. It made no practical sense to Murray to take tax dollars from the industrious and give it to the less industrious. In other words, income transfers that took money from the rich and gave it to the poor made no sense from policy standpoint. For Murray, it was simply morally wrong to develop social welfare polices and programs, that, through income transfers, made it rational for the poor to quit working and use welfare benefits as a basis for choosing to increase the size of their families or have children in the first place. In chapter 17 of *Losing Ground* Murray proposed a thought experiment that has been the springboard for welfare reform in 1996. He simply said:

> our final and most ambitious thought experiment, consists of scrapping the entire federal welfare and income-support structure for working-aged persons, including AFDC, Medicaid, Food Stamps, Unemployment Insurance, subsidized housing, disability insurance and the rest. It would leave the working aged person with no other recourse whatsoever except the job market, family members, friends, and public or private locally funded local services. It is the Alexandrian solution: cut the knot for there is no way to untie it (Murray 1984 pp: 227–28).

Just whose ideas were these scholars fighting anyway? To get a glimpse of this, we have to go back to the authoritative 1958 book by Harold Wilensky and Charles Lebeaux, *Industrial Society and Social Welfare*, a work whose ideas, almost without debate, shaped the underpinnings of welfare policy development until the 1980s. To understand the welfare debate that has gone on since the 1980s it is important to realize that t' vo competing perspectives of welfare outlined in that work representeu an ideological militarized zone. Those perspectives were not just about redistribution. They were also about the nature of the human being in relationship to the market place. The first view, called the *residual perspective*, and minimized by Wilensky, Lebeaux, and other liberal university scholars, was the position that Murray, Gilder, and later other conservative thinkers were championing. It was a perspective that had lost its favor with the public from the New Deal to the 1980s:

> The *residual perspective* is based on the premise that there are two natural channels through which an individual's needs are met: the family and the market economy. These are the preferred structures of supply. When there is a breakdown in these institutions, family life is disrupted by the death of the bread winner, a depression causes unexpected unemployment, or the person cannot make normal use of the channels, because of illness or old age, a third mechanism is brought into play—the welfare structure. This is conceived as a residual agency attending to primarily emergency functions and is expected to withdraw when the regular social structure—the family or the economic system are working properly. Because of its residual, temporary, substitute characteristic, thus conceived, often carries the stigma of the dole or charity. (Wilensky and Lebeaux 1958: 138)

When the calls for the religious community to become increasingly involved in welfare reform from the Reagan years on are examined closely, it is obvious they are rooted in the residual perspective in two ways. First, there is a hint that people who usually fail in the marketplace ("a preferred structure of supply"), and slide into poverty, may do so because of a lack of moral strength. And second, if they cannot help themselves, or their families cannot help them out of their moral and impoverished bind, then the church can both address the moral cause and help with the concrete provision of services until those in need are able to find their own way. In either instance, this perspective's built-in solution is logically found through the voluntary efforts of the faith community.

The other view, and the one promoted by Wilensky, Lebeaux, and other liberal thinkers was the *institutional perspective*, and it puts matters quite differently:

> The *institutional perspective* is defined as the organized system of social services and institutions, designed to aid individuals and groups attain satisfying standards of life and health. It aims at personal and social relationships which permit individuals the fullest development of their capacities and promotion of their well being in harmony with the needs of the community. This definition of the institutional view implies no stigma, no emergency, no abnormalcy. Social welfare becomes accepted as a proper, legitimate function of modern industrial society in helping individuals achieve self fulfillment. The complexity of modern life is recognized. The inability of the individual to provide fully for himself or meet all his needs in family and work settings is considered a "normal" condition; and the helping agencies achieve regular institutional status (Wilensky and Lebeaux 1958: 139 and 140).

An important difference between the scholars who championed conservative causes and those who championed the liberal ones was that conservative intellectuals quickly learned to use mainstream print, electronic media, and later on, the Internet, to bring their concerns to the public.

Ironically, the liberal and moderate scholars from the universities, whose ideas in the 1950s, 1960s, and 1970s dominated the public discussion, remained conservative by steadfastly subjecting their scholarship to the tests of anonymous review by their colleagues in the academy before going public. (It is important to note that the press does not have the capability to test the intellectual merit of good or bad research. It reports news of research findings as if such findings are fact, when the facts may be suspect [Wineburg 1987]). That is a time-consuming task, to say the least, which often kept them at a disadvantage in influencing fast-paced policy changes and the corresponding public policy debates throughout the 1980s.

Now, after more than two decades of an ideological public warfare, right wing thinkers have come to dominate the national policy debate. The list of public issues that has emerged from conservative policy factories, as Michael Shuman (1998) has called them, is a long one: term limits, unfunded mandates, school vouchers, the balanced budget amendment, workfare (from which welfare reform evolved), the flat tax, right to work, free trade agreements, enterprise zones, commercial free speech, and more. As Shuman (1998) goes on to point out, the multi-issue conservative think tanks funded by right-leaning foundations have enabled conservative public scholars to present a clear and compelling story about the failures of big government which much of the American public has now accepted.

The ideas of Gilder and Murray, in less than two decades, have become accepted widely by the public and have served as the cornerstones of current social welfare policy in Washington and on Main Street. On one hand, Gilder championed an unfettered free market, and more importantly for this discussion, made popular the idea that welfare provisions caused the breakdown in families. On the other, Murray, with mountains of data, tried to prove the point that social welfare programs themselves caused a growth in welfare, and that welfare was an incentive for women to have out-of-wedlock births.

Before going too far in this discussion, it is essential for me to note that causality is a difficult thing to pinpoint, especially in the political and social environment. Corporate welfare, a set of income transfers that goes from the taxpayers to wealthy individuals and corporations, has skyrocketed, but interestingly, we don't chronicle the out-of-wedlock births, marriages, divorces, and fecundity rates for the recipients of those subsidies, and we probably won't. No one really believes that sexual habits and birth control practices of such people have anything to do with a tobacco subsidy or huge tax write-off for a legislator's favorite corporation. From my vantage point, the welfare debate has been less about the truth, and more about winning an ideological debate about the distribution of resources in society. What Gilder and Murray were really fighting against were the liberal notions of welfare that had a strong redistribution element to them. In other words, they thought that transferring income to the poor made them weak, lazy, and promiscuous.

Just about everything in the set of residual relationships is voluntary, and that notion keeps in tune with the tenor of conservative thinking. The conservative view of welfare sees people being responsible for their actions and when an unforeseen event disables them from proper individual, social, or economic functioning, temporary help by public or private means would be available. When I talk later on about the push from the politicians toward more local service development and religious involvement, it should be remembered that those ideas are coming from the residual perspective.

The institutional perspective has dominated social welfare policy and development since the Great Depression. Nevertheless, its elements, as I will point out later, have been rooted in local service design and delivery since nationhood, and not so surprisingly, so have the elements of its residual counterpart. Yet, in their prediction that the institutional perspective would become predominant, Wilensky and Lebeaux set up a false division between the two perspectives, and by making this division, they may have vilified the important dimensions of the residual perspective. Corresponding service development for the last twenty-plus years was based on the institutional view. The human being in this framework was cast as an actor who could be as much a victim of a changing tide of social circumstances as master of his or her own fate. As a consequence, government had the responsibility to support the victims of circumstance in the form of programs.

A major problem with the domination of the institutional view was that its adherents basically ignored the complex set of partnerships among all the actors in the local system of services. It set up federal programs for every problem, making the public and private local systems hard to understand, harder to manage, and still harder to coordinate. With some understanding and appreciation of the private, residual infrastructure of local services, they could have used federal funds to enhance that system instead of adding federal program after federal program. The domination of the federal programs, while well-intended, sometimes submerged the effectiveness of local service delivery efforts. The Reagan budget cuts of the 1980s addressed this problem by eliminating more than a hundred categorical federal programs, recasting them into twelve block grants, and sending them back to the states with less money.

The message was clear that those government programs were an administrative nightmare and that local communities could do more with less. The cuts of the 1980s were swift and dramatic and gave no time for the supporting private agencies, religious congregations, and charities to plan for an appropriate transition. While the budget knife by no means cut all the

programs, the policy sent a loud and clear public message: government programs are ineffective; private programs are better. Because of the mass of
programs and services, critics who merely saw a service boondoggle failed
to recognize and publicly pronounce programmatic successes which
included the virtual elimination of abject poverty among the elderly by way
of the Food Stamp program; Medicaid and Medicare; and the programs
included in the federal Older American's Act; Social Security and SSI; an
end to child malnutrition that especially plagued the South in the 1960s
when programs like Food Stamps, School Lunch and Breakfast programs,
and prenatal programs like Women, Infants, and Children (WIC) were first
implemented (Kammer 1997). So the ideological wars between the liberals
and conservatives heated up while the workers in the public agencies who
had to solve local problems scrambled to do more with less.

As I will demonstrate extensively in chapter 4, residual social services
like self-help and religiously based service programs were now called on to
collaborate with financially disabled public or institutional services to solve
community problems. While merging of institutional and residual efforts
locally has always been the real way that service delivery evolved in this
country, churches especially stepped up their efforts in a huge way in the
Reagan years, so much so that the calls now for more religious involvement
in social service seem somewhat disingenuous. The irony here is that maybe
the religious right was really talking to itself.

A substantial portion of this book will argue the following point: The
ideological debate over what perspective ought to dominate the design and
delivery of social welfare has obscured a real understanding of the complex
realities of the nature of the problems of poverty, and how the ever-evolv-
ing interwoven system of social services work at the local level. I want to
point out that the increasing prominence of the perspective of Gilder and
especially Murray, who toyed with ending all institutional services, has created a fantasy-like analysis that when implemented as it is now being done
in communities everywhere, will cause increasing chaos. When such thinking evolves into programs, such as what happened when the institutional
view did not take into account the validity of the residual perspective in
service design and development, it wreaks havoc for the practitioners and
recipients of service. As I will illustrate later, the social problems and the
system of intertwined social service institutions at the local level are not
abstract entities belonging to one or another ideological camp. Failure to

understand the local terrain by both liberal and conservative architects of social welfare has contributed significantly to both policy perspectives always coming under harsh attack by adherents of the other camp. In reality, the admixture of the "institutional" and "residual" is what constitutes the main ingredients of the unique social service system in the United States.

So, instead of my staking out an unshakable ideological position, I will ultimately be calling for a coherent policy that strengthens the partnerships at the local level among agencies who go back and forth in service design and delivery between the residual and institutional views. Today's welfare reform policy gives a recipient a total of five years of federal support. The ideas underscoring that policy thrust are rooted in the *residual perspective* of welfare and are clearly statements against the ideas in the *institutional policy perspective* that had dominated welfare development. Remember, the old institutional view shaped policy so that a mother was guaranteed a lifetime of minimal public financial support. It was assumed from that perspective as a "normal" condition, that the complexity of modern life would sometimes make the individual unable to fully provide for herself or meet all her needs in the family.

Thus, the helping agencies, or the welfare bureaucracy as it is called today, achieved regular institutional status. The current twist here is that in the new world of social services policy, a recipient now *cannot* receive public welfare after five years. If she finds employment, but her wages are low enough for federal food assistance, she *could* continue with food stamps and Medicaid (with some qualification), two public and institutional programs. If her wages are too low to support her food needs even with food stamps, current reports are indicating that she is increasingly using local food pantries which are often religiously based. Accordingly, the local social service system now has to adjust to food and medical needs of a woman who does not make it in this new policy scheme and will now also have to do tremendous work in helping her meet the financial needs of her family if she does not make it in the market place. Unfortunately, as a practical matter, she now has to interact with two instead of three public programs, but many private ones if she cannot make ends meet. The locality now has to construct an entirely new system of services to handle the problems caused by a shifting policy. And who is being leaned on to solve these problems? The religious community.

While Gilder and Murray's ideas were making their way into the public discourse, and eventually came to dominate policy thought, something else very important was taking place. The calls for new polices centering on getting the federal government out of public welfare never mentioned how such actions would affect the design and delivery of local services except in the most general terms: local people know how to solve their own problems and could do so if left alone by the bureaucrats in Washington. The philosophy articulated by the intellectual right, on the one hand, called for a return to the days when neighbors helped each other with a spirit of brotherhood that by its very nature was a spirit unfettered by federal intervention. On the other hand, its implementation, something few have studied, slammed local systems of services, by withdrawing support, and also by changing the nature of the complex interrelationships among the well-intended actors in the system of local services trying their best to help the needy even when they were the targets of attacks that they had little chance of refuting.

Now, the new welfare reform of this era, with a fresh twist, intends to keep food and medical services in place for the poor. Yet, it forces local systems with no more resources than they had prior to the cuts to finance people who are no longer entitled to help. It makes no difference whether the reasons are a result of their own doing, or reasons beyond their control. The religious community, whose services are best characterized as residual in nature, are now being asked to develop both institutional and residual services for mothers. For example, on the institutional side, it is being asked to be the permanent job retention arm of this new policy. On the residual side, the faith community is being summoned to finance those who don't make it in the workforce because of the assumed moral flaw in their character. The ramifications of the overall policy won't be known for years, but the system of service locally is in transformation.

The budget cuts of the 1980s stimulated, as I will demonstrate in the following chapters, a large increase by the religious community in local volunteering and support of the nonprofit and public agencies in the local system of services. I will show that the religious community was instrumental in preventing the needy from going deeper into poverty in the 1980s. It helped its local system of services to survive a recession, budget cuts, and manage new social problems like AIDS and homelessness.

Nevertheless, those cuts of the 1980s also hindered the ability of local service systems to solve or prevent many of the social problems that plague us today. The systems locally became holding bays for managing difficult problems that seemingly had no solutions. It took until the 1990s for local service systems to recover from the huge cuts of the 1980s, and for practitioners to create a new logic and method of doing things. I will explore this idea more fully later. Policy pundits and scholars alike have not understood that local social service systems, in urban and even in rural areas, are complex, interwoven channels of public and private care, quite often undergirded by the exchange of resources, ideas, and services. The local systems develop their own logic, norms, and cultures and have created numerous partnerships.

There probably is no single perspective that provides an accurate way of seeing the system of services in a local community. The institutional view allows for an understanding of the array of federal, state, and local public programs while the residual perspective allows us to understand the rise of numerous self-help groups, and programs that have emerged out of religious congregations. Yet neither view alone allows for an understanding of how some programs start out to be voluntary and residual, but evolve into public and institutional programs actually keeping religious vestiges or, in the current case of welfare reform, devolve into residual and institutional hybrids. There are important residual *and* institutional types of programs that are providing for the broader social stability.

In chapter 7, I will show that this trend is neither liberal nor conservative any longer, but merely a practical outcome of modern social service life. The way a local system of services meets personal and social needs which permit individuals the fullest development and promotes well-being and harmony in the context of community needs is accomplished through shared voluntary efforts, contracting of services from public and private agencies, religious congregations, interagency meetings, community forums, and the like. Sometimes the contracts are formal and financial and sometimes they are informal arrangements. For example, when a public entity such as a department of public health experiences a huge budget cut in child health care, the problems that were paid for by the funds that got eliminated do not go away. They often fester and then get reassigned to other community agencies.

The budget cuts of the Reagan years created a gigantic shift in resources flowing from the religious community into the general community of local social care and made congregations increasingly key to local service provision and holding the community together. Without tremendous congregational support what would communities have looked like? It is a fair question to ask in this new policy climate that is trying to reimpose a residual system of services on communities.

Contrary to what the conservative right may be thinking, the religious community played a major role in helping to create a new and dynamic set of interconnections locally. Those interconnections went largely unnoticed because mainline congregations, not those that lined up with the conservative right, stepped in and helped without much fanfare. Just as the system developed a logic and coherence from the cuts in the 1980s, the momentum of the ideas of the right increased the strain on local systems, and even more demands were placed on the religious community.

Throughout this book, I will call for partnerships at the local level among all of the actors in a system of services that tries to bring about well-being for people in need. It will be important to understand the difference between the rhetoric behind the calls for changing welfare and the reality facing the system of services, and how that system actually operates.

CHAPTER ONE

Devolution or Devilution

I took my 17-year-old son with me when I conducted my interviews at Salvation Army Headquarters and Catholic Charities USA in the summer of 1997, figuring I'd teach the kid the tricks of the trade. At the end of my interview at Catholic Charities, I asked Zach if he had any questions, just as I did the day before at Salvation Army. He asked: "What is devolution?" In the middle of my academic definition of programs being sent back to the states and local level, he said, "Oh, I thought you meant *devil*ution." Maybe I did.

❐

FIVE MAJOR POINTS OF CHAPTER 1

Focus

1. As conservative scholars became more influential in shaping the ideas concerning welfare policy development, it became easier for the religious language of good and evil to shroud the pubic discourse of welfare during the 1980s and 1990s.
2. The good and evil language of welfare grew out of a right wing religious tradition in this country. Consequently, welfare policy was shaped increasingly by politicians whose constituents were on the religious right.
3. It was, however, the mainline religious groups who increasingly delivered services brought by budget cuts, but the public discourse about welfare drifted rightward.

4. There is a long tradition of religious service delivery in this country, and such traditions are embedded in local service systems. As the programs and services become even more localized, we will see more of the mainline religious service providers shaping the local public discourse, because of their long involvement in providing goods and services locally. Much of the scholarship has ignored service delivery—a key to understand how a policy works.
5. The political discourse about welfare has not reflected the complex matters facing providers and recipients, so policy development in this latest era in social service development is on flimsy grounds.

❏

An earlier version of this chapter appears in Ram A. Cnaan with Robert J. Wineburg and Stephanie C. Boddie. 1999. *The Newer Deal: Social Work and Religion in Partnership.* New York: Columbia University Press. The context is different in that Cnaan's work redevelops the intellectual history of Social Work while the work here looks at a two decade development of the religious community's response to welfare policy.

THE DEVIL IN DEVILUTION

An important question facing scholar and practitioner alike is: How has conservative thinking and its rhetoric, often characterized as right-wing American religion, shaped the design and delivery of social services? It is an essential question because the religious community is central to the success or failure of a new welfare reform policy that hands much of the design and delivery of welfare services to states and localities. While leaders of both political parties have called for more religious involvement in solving social problems, nearly a quarter century after the Reagan budget cuts there is still no single piece of scholarship that analyzes the impact the social policy decisions of the Reagan years had on social service systems in local communities. As a consequence, there is little guidance for informing our understanding of the current policy of devolution of welfare services which is arguably the most profound change in social service policy in more than sixty years. Local systems of service will undoubtedly be stretched even further than they are at present in order to provide day care, transportation, transitional funds, employment training, and other supports. The changes will not necessarily produce a better system, but they will certainly thwart comprehensive service development.

Despite the sparse research, the existing work can be greatly illuminated by taking a look at how and why the media portrayed the people and organizations that grabbed the public's attention while the major changes were taking place locally. This is, of course, a legitimate but awkward approach to scholarly investigation. Reporters usually do not have a broad background in the field they are writing about nor do they have the space in their columns to give stories the attention that scholars might give them. What you may get may not be all that there is. On the other hand, news stories are about real people and capture the events of the moment and they shape the public's view of things.

The limited research, which I'll discuss more fully in the next chapter, indeed shows that religious congregations and charities responded to President Reagan's budget cuts and that their community service activities grew. Today, ready or not, the forces behind "devolution" or handing programs once run by the federal government back to states and localities, have done precisely that. I will show that when localities received this baton it was slapped hardest into the palms of the religious community. How exactly did we get here and what does it mean?

THE RELIGIOUS RIGHT

In order to grasp on how the intellectual ideas of the conservative right, especially those of Gilder and Murray among others, took hold, it is important to see them converging with the ideas of the religious right which were also making their way into the public discourse. Two televangelists, Reverends Jerry Falwell and Pat Robertson, were instrumental in softening the environment for conservative Christianity's increasingly visible role in politics in the early 1980s, and for its evolution into the moral architect of welfare reform in the mid-1990s. Falwell, leader of the political action group known as The Moral Majority and pastor of Thomas Road Baptist Church in Lynchburg, Virginia, rose to dominate the print and electronic media during the 1980s. He helped shape the Reagan Administration's social agenda in the 1980s (Willis 1990). Falwell is especially important because he blurred the lines of church and state by appearing publicly with Republican politicians early in the Reagan years. In turn, moderates and even some liberals increasingly became influenced by Falwell and then Reverend Pat Robertson's political action group, the Christian Coalition in the 1990s.

Falwell and Robertson had a spirit like that of evangelist Dwight Moody who, one hundred years earlier, saw himself as a lifeboat in a world of wrecked vessels. There is one major difference. To Moody, any organized effort to improve society was a distraction from winning souls (Marty 1980). To Falwell and Robertson, it was important to work with government to put society back on track. Their aim was to cleanse an immoral public and return government, despite a supposed separation of church and state, to its Christian roots. Their message became part of the public discourse and ultimately undergirded the moral grounds for formation of the current public welfare policy laid out in the intellectual sphere by Murray, Gilder, and later on Lawrence Mead and Robert Rector. The problem was twofold: the lack of individual responsibility on the part of the welfare recipient, and the welfare bureaucracy.

Few would have guessed in the early 1980s that Falwell's message was anything more than a blip in welfare history, let alone the first steps of movement with Republican politicians that would ultimately lead to a Contract With America that rolled federal welfare services back to the states and localities.

If we go back just a few years in history, we can see how Ronald Reagan set the tone for public discussions and development of social policy. It evolved for more than thirty years, and for many of those years ran counter to the language that underscored the welfare policy developments in the 1960s and 1970s. In Reagan's nomination speech of Barry Goldwater in 1964, "A Time for Choosing"(a.k.a. *The Speech*), Reagan provides a context for using the good and evil" language of religion to characterize the poor and the state-designed programs and services to help them. The excerpt below captures some of that language.

> We are faced with the most evil enemy mankind has ever known from his long climb from swamp to stars. There can be no security anywhere in the free world if there is no fiscal and economic security within the United States. Those who ask us to trade our freedom for the *soup kitchen of the welfare state* [my emphasis] are architects of a policy of accommodation (Reagan Home Page, 1997).

In that speech, the evil Reagan refers to is, of course, the former Soviet Union. But the internal enemy is our ever-growing welfare state. Reagan knew that if he was going to replace that welfare state with church-run soup kitchens, church and state ultimately needed to get together. Eighteen years later, in a 1982 speech to clergy, including Reverend Jerry Falwell, now President Reagan had honed his language to make his message unmistakable about poverty and the pathway out of it.

An April 14, 1982 story in the *Washington Post*, by Herbert Denton, chronicled those first public movements. The story, titled "Reagan Urges More Church Aid for Needy," noted that at a luncheon speech in the State Dining Room, President Reagan told that group of more than 100 religious leaders "*that churches and voluntary groups should accept more responsibility for the needy rather than leaving it to the bureaucracy* (emphasis mine)." President Reagan had created a public devil—"the government bureaucrat"—and a public model—the Good Samaritan. President Reagan, possibly receiving his cues from Falwell, went on in that meeting to deliver commentary on the Good Samaritan to the clergy gathered there:

> The story of the Good Samaritan has always illustrated to me what God's challenge really is. He crossed the road, knelt down, bound up the wounds of the beaten traveler, the pilgrim and carried him to the nearest town. He didn't go running into town and look for a caseworker to tell him that there was a fellow out there that needed help. He took it upon himself (Denton, 1982, Reagan Home Page, 1997)[1].

In so doing, the president created a new way of defining the causes of poverty. This new metaphor instantly undercut the liberal view of poverty that pointed to failures in large systems like government, the marketplace, or schools as a major causes of poverty. Reagan strengthened conservative interpretations that the causes of poverty were in personal character flaws and government operated social programs. His administration paved the way to let federal and state tax revenue pour more easily than ever before into religious charities and congregations.

Besides Falwell, members of that group of religious leaders included Catholic representative Cardinal Terrence Cooke and heads of many major religious denominations, several of whom dissented from the president's focus. They had gathered earlier for meetings with members of The Presidential Task Force on Private Sector Initiatives. Cardinal Cooke's presence is noteworthy because as the gathering's representative of one of Christianity's oldest, and its largest denominations, which includes 16,000 churches in the United States and more than 1,200 charities, it was important politically that he agreed with the president. He was given the honor of presenting the luncheon invocation through which he tempered the atmosphere by saying there was a role both for the *government* and the *churches* and *citizens* to minister to the poor. Quite often since then, most Catholic leaders in the welfare debate have been on the opposite side from the religious right, because Catholics are far more involved in social service provision locally around the country than most evangelical Christians (see table 1.1). Consequently, they have come to different interpretations about the causes and remedies for poverty.

In choreographing those first steps, President Reagan paved the way for the most dramatic reversal in social welfare policy since the 1930s. The New Deal policies of President Franklin Roosevelt had shifted social service design and delivery away from a primarily local, voluntary, and somewhat religiously based system to one that by 1980 would be dominated by government programs at each level—federal, state, and local. Reagan's early meeting with those religious leaders was the catalyst that sent American religion, with regard to local social service design and delivery in the 1980s and 1990s, in two distinct directions.

On the religious and political right were the clerics, politicians, and scholars from conservative think tanks, all of whom shaped the political discourse around the causes and effects of welfare. The intellectual, ideological, and rhetorical parameters of the policy debate were sketched most forcefully and artistically by the works of George Gilder and Charles Mur-

---

Table 1.1

Catholics in Detroit Do More, as 1982 Correspondence from
Catholic Service Providers to President Reagan Demonstrates

An interesting sidebar to this split appears in a September, 1982 Charities USA, a publication of the National Conference of Catholic Charities. The article is called "A letter to President Reagan from Two Vincentains (And the White House reply.") The May 13th 1982 letter, by Oliver Wendt, President, and Partick Adamick, Executive Secretary of Society of St. Vincent DePaul Central Council of Detroit. The letter demonstrates the increase in demand for services from 1980 to 1981 as shown below. The letter also then calls for input from organizations like themselves in shaping the policy of cutbacks.

Funds Expended For	1981	1980	% of increase
Food	$209,237	$157,037	33
Rent	45,122	33,616	34
Utilities	35,637	27,534	29
Transportation	11,161	4,459	150
Medical Care	11,449	8,818	30

The White House Reply was a 10 line response that thanks them for their concern, notes that the Reagan administration is "dedicated to encouraging a higher level of individual initiative," and tells them to keep up the good work.

ray. Gilder's *Wealth and Poverty* (1981) and Murray's *Losing Ground* (1984 [1983]) represented the first scholarly attempts from the conservative right to change the policy debate about the causes and cures of poverty.

The moral parameters of social policy debate and discussion were drawn by the Christian right. They captured the media and political attention and shaped the terms of the welfare discussion. But for those fourteen years leading up to the passage of the current welfare reform law, *the actual provision of social services* brought about by the cuts of the Reagan and Bush administrations had increasingly *become the domain of mainline American religious denominations like the Catholics* as noted above, and not by churches who aligned themselves with Falwell and Robertson.

Among those mainline denominations were the African Methodists Episcopalians (AME), American Baptists, Black Baptists, Catholics, Episcopalians, Jews, Lutherans, Methodists, Presbyterians, Unitarians, members of United Church of Christ. The Salvation Army is one major exception to trend of the evangelicals shaping policy on the one hand, and the mainline denominations delivering it on the other. The Salvation Army is a theologically strong evangelical Christian church that has stayed out of the political spotlight. Yet in the 1995–96 welfare reform debate, it publicly came out against the reforms adapted by Congress and turned into law (Kammer 1997). The Army has, however, remained in the center of social service design and delivery, as it had been, for 116 years, before the Reagan era. What makes The Salvation Army different from other evangelicals is that their motto "soup, soap, and salvation" is based deeply on The Salvation Army's founder General William General William Booth's sincere belief that the life of Christ required His children to relieve the misery of their fellow beings. In his famous Cab-Horse Charter he makes the case for helping relieve people's misery. The General denounced the fact that the poor in London in the mid-1800s were not

> [G]enerally . . . as well cared for as horses. When a cab horse falls no one faults the creature for being weary or careless, or stupid; he is helped to his feet at once, for his own sake and to prevent an obstruction to traffic. And more: once back on his feet, he is given work, fed, kept warm and dry at night. These then are the two points of the Cab-Horse Charter. When he is down he is helped up, and while he lives he has food, shelter and work (Begbie 1920: 92).

WELFARE AS WE KNEW IT

Sectarian welfare services throughout the 1980s were delivered by the Salvation Army and other mainline congregations and charities. While the religious right pushed welfare reform back to the states, localities, and to faith communities whether they were ready or not, the Christian Coalition and supporters, unlike their Salvationists and mainline Christian brethren, had not delivered much of the nation's sectarian social services. The budget of the Christian Coalition is about $25 million (Birnbaum 1995) as opposed to a total of $1.9 billion in the budgets of the 1,200 Catholic Charities around the country (Brogioli, 1997 personal conversation) and the $1.4 billion of the 1,200 local churches of The Salvation Army Corps[2] nationwide. It is interesting to note that the people who give the goods, provide the service, and offer strength to their neighbors have had less to say in shaping the values of current welfare policy than people with larger budgets spent on shaping the social and moral policy agenda. In a June 1997 interview I had with Major Tom Jones, Director of Development and Community Relations of the Salvation Army nationally, I was told that there is more demand than the Army can meet in this thriving economy. Some local corps at that time were running deficits which had not been the case historically for the U.S. Salvation Army.

The Salvation Army has an extensive network of services and programs, many of which are collaborative efforts with public agencies, supported by clergy, human service professionals, and faithful volunteers. Yet it cannot meet needs. How then are we going to enlist newcomers to the field? How will we build a structure of thoughtful and effective service efforts or raise funds or recruit volunteers? How will we coordinate and evaluate our programs without creating a nightmare at the local level?

Before we ask too many questions, a brief look back into history—the history of local service systems—will reveal that they always had a religious influence, and that public, private, and religious partnerships have been evolving for years. Three essential points emerge which will make it easier to view both how the Reagan cuts of the 1980s changed the local system of services, and what we might expect of the new cuts.

First, social service provision in this country, at the local level, has always had a religious and public connection, and historically not much fuss was made about it. Second, the church and state connection, in different eras of American history, has expanded and contracted, much like an accordion. We have never been without the connection. As a result, some of the models of partnership among the various actors in the local system of services have come at different times in our nation's history of service development. For example, The Red Cross began in my community in 1917. It has provided a *social service* function by offering emergency relief to people. It has played a *community education* role by educating citizens on everything from water safety to AIDS prevention. And it has provided a *public health* function by collecting and distributing blood. Since its inception here, three members of the clergy have been members of its board of director's executive committee. This means that in eighty years of the Red Cross's life in Greensboro, it has had representation from most of congregations in the community on its executive committee of the board. The congregations and the Red Cross are like cousins. When I saw a Red Cross Bloodmobile with its huge red cross parked next the Beth David Synagogue sign, I did not blink. It is the way things are supposed to be with cousins even in an interfaith service marriage. The current policy changes simply reflect another phase of development, where the religious community—along with local public agencies, private nonprofits, self-help groups, and even for-profit providers—will continue to carve out new relations, and enhance mature ones.

Third, large social policies like the new welfare reform play out at the local level. The current calls for increased religious involvement to make up for the cuts in governmental programs, as I alluded to a while ago, usually come with very little understanding of how local communities organize or operate their public and private social services, and how the voluntary coordination and cooperation among religious and secular providers works. The result has been the development of policy based on a misunderstanding of what the religious community can and cannot accomplish. As long as I can remember, the public discourse around the "welfare system" has centered on its being characterized as top heavy, distant, and unresponsive. Yet, in each era, the system of services through which welfare and social services are delivered has developed an internal consistency and a way of operating that the recipients and providers understand. Most people would agree that the system now being the reformed was flawed and needed overhauling precisely because its recipients knew the loopholes. In addition, the public's perception of program personnel (the bureaucrats and caseworkers) has been that they could not deliver services effectively, and this turned them into social service cops instead of people who are truly caring and are concerned for the needy. Part of this view is true, but only part.

In my twenty years in North Carolina, I have taught more than one thousand students, many of whom staff the TANF (former AFDC) foster care, adoption, and child-and-adult protection divisions of the public bureaucracies in our state. They also work in public health agencies, mental health agencies, and public schools. Many of my former students are hard-working mainstream Christians who see their casework as an expression of their faith. There are many more such dedicated caseworkers than one might expect. When the people they serve cannot make ends meet, they enlist their churches to cushion the real pain that they see daily (Wineburg, 1996). Welfare personnel are, in many instances, the Good Samaritans.

The important thing to remember is that the successful transition to an administratively small, approachable, and accountable social service system must be accompanied by comprehensive local service planning, a spirit of cooperation, an understanding of the complexities of poverty, and an accurate and sober analysis of the system's *current* capability to serve. This must be coupled with a thoughtful assessment of what new contributors like congregations or religious charities might offer each other in new or maturing partnerships. Local service systems by their design are not equipped to do that kind of planning well because they react to problems; they do not, by nature, prevent them. Nor are local service systems doing very much with regard to long-range planning. Agencies get their funds by demonstrating they meet needs. But diverting funds, staff time, and other agency and community resources to long-range planning efforts that require demonstrating that the actual *planning* effort itself contributed to the decrease in a problem is at best trying to demonstrate something on flimsy ground, and has little organizational payoff. If a local system needs to be reoriented or changed, the first step will be to get a sober analysis of local issues and group local institutions to take on the long-range planning endeavor. This first step should involve the academic community and could be coupled with a process of educating the community on the nature and scope of local problems.

HISTORICAL CONNECTION

If local citizens, clergy, agency planners, or scholars choose to look closely at the evolution of human services in communities across the United States, they would find that the path has been laid for bringing religious, government, and private nonprofit agencies to the planning table. There has been a changing but continuous history of religious activity in cooperation with government and private agencies helping people in need. In pre-revolutionary Virginia, for example, municipal poor law officials already serving as Anglican church officials cared for the old, the sick, the deserted, and the illegitimate children of their communities (Coll 1973). Religiously inspired institutions in the Pennsylvania colony, notably the Pennsylvania Hospital and the Philadelphia Bettering House, jointly financed by taxation and private contributions, offered unsurpassed facilities for treating the sick and sheltering the poor (Bremner 1960; I am citing the 6th ed. of 1972).

The Quakers, active today worldwide in social causes, founded The Friends Almshouse in Philadelphia in 1713 to support the community's destitute (Axinn and Levin, 1982). During colonial times, some religious societies relieved public officials of the necessity for caring for their community's poor by supplying mutual aid to members and dispensing charity to certain categories of beneficiaries (Bremner 1960).

Reverend S. Humphreys Gurteen, who drew on the model of the London Charity Organization of the Episcopal clergy, began a Charity Organization Society in Buffalo, New York in 1877. Friendly visiting of the poor by church volunteers was the essence of this movement in the United States. The movement became known as the new benevolent gospel (Schweinitz 1943; I am citing the paperback edition of 1975). Social welfare historian Roy Lubove (1965: 13–14) captures the broader significance of this movement and the importance of the voluntary spirit of the church volunteer when he notes: "The society without the volunteer visitors was little better than a charitable machine lacking moral purpose and unfit for the fundamental task of helping the poor to help themselves." Faith Matters, a program I present in chapter 9, has vestiges of this spirit. In the early twentieth century, when relief became more formal and secularized, the moral guidance approach of the volunteer visitors was replaced by the new and growing profession known as social work. Nevertheless, while social work and other helping professions took secular forms, congregational involvement did not vanish even though little scholarly attention was paid to the religious influence on service development.

Some of today's better known organizations with religious beginnings, like the United Way and the Child Welfare League, long ago shed the outward signs of their religious origin (Reid and Stimpson 1983). However, some religious organizations begun in the 1800s, most notably the YMCA, the YWCA, and the Salvation Army (a church in the Methodist tradition), have not only retained their religious heritage, but are also essential to the planning and delivery of human service systems in many communities. Without this long and unbroken tradition of local service involvement, it is unlikely that the outpouring of assistance to the homeless, hungry, and other groups by local religious congregations nationwide during the 1980s and continuing today could have transpired with such speed and relative uniformity.

CONTINUITY AMIDST CHANGE

Welfare historian Roy Lubove (1992) helps us usnderstand how social change happens historically by stressing that it is essential to understand how institutions often keep some continuity with the past while also changing to meet present social conditions. For example, congregations were this country's first social welfare institutions. Yet, as noted above, even before nationhood, congregations were intertwined with public bodies to bring about community social welfare. As American society moved from a rural and agricultural economic base to an urban and industrial foundation, congregations and religious leaders remained instrumental in developing voluntary organizations to meet the needs of a new urban scene. At the beginning of the twentieth century, when efforts to help the poor became more formal and secularized, the moral guidance approach of volunteer visitors was replaced by the new and growing profession known as social work (Lubove 1965).

When the Great Depression spawned a major development in the welfare state as we know it, congregations took on a clearer subsidiary welfare function in communities. They developed their foreign missions and denominational organizational structures (Johnson 1956), but they were no longer capable of being a major partner with local governments and non-profits in providing the social welfare function for their communities and the society. Congregations, however, did not stop their development or abort their subsidiary welfare function; they just were not the main partners in the provision of local services. From a perspective of continuity amidst change, the role congregations now play in providing community welfare has changed from the past, but their continuous historical social welfare function is clear. Congregations were poised to take on new roles as the combination of the Reagan and Bush retrenchment policies and new problems like AIDS and homelessness strapped local communities. We have much to learn from how communities responded to the Reagan era cuts. And we have much to learn about the real partnerships that shape the local service community. But a question that needs answering next is just where has the academic community been while all these changes have taken place and why haven't they been a force in these changes? Why haven't they carried out a policy and service debate in the press with scholars on the right? It is clear that if scholarship is going to exorcise the devil from the loose and tangential analysis of current welfare reform, or *devilution* as my son called it, they will have to study the details of local service provision.

CHAPTER TWO

A Blip in History or a Slip in the Academy?

In 1987, I presented a paper on the emerging role of religious congregations in social service delivery at a prestigious university. At lunch, I told a prominent historian that I thought that religious involvement in social service would be a very important social service concern in the 1990s. I was told with a yawn that religious involvement and the Reagan budget cuts were but blips in history. In an August 25, 1997 *Time* story by Adam Cohen called "Feeding the Flock," Cohen, like Ronald Reagan some 15 years earlier, dismisses the entire public service efforts in welfare in one half of a line. " . . . government is increasingly asking churches to succeed where social workers and government bureaucrats handing out checks have failed."

❐

SUMMARY: MAJOR POINTS OF CHAPTER 2

Focus of Chapter Two.

1. We do not have an overarching analysis of the role the religious community plays in the system of services at the local level.
2. The academic community has not been geared up to study local matters, while the Reagan budget cuts turned service design and delivery increasingly local.

3. Religious leaders and politicians, increasingly from both political persuasions, and without the help of much academic research, defined the problems and put forth the solutions.
4. Their analysis was more in line with the popular metaphors noted in chapter 1 than a sober assessment of the problem and conscientious solutions that sometimes emerge from careful academic investigation.

❏

THE ACADEMIC COMMUNITY

During the 1980s the scholarly community virtually ignored one of the most important changes to hit local human service systems in many years—the way the Reagan administration's budget cuts in human services stimulated the formation and maturation of partnerships between the religious community and local service providers. Even though the academy paid very little attention, we know enough to say with assurance that those cuts altered the way communities delivered human services permanently. Today, scholars are trying to understand the implications of welfare reform as major responsibilities shift from the federal level to states and localities (devolution). Many are now trying to make sense out of the calls for churches to deliver more social services. That won't happen without taking into account how the changes affect the local system of services.

In the introduction to his book *Welfare in America: Christian Perspectives on a Policy in Crisis* (1996), Stanley Carlson-Thies captures the long-standing, central tenet of American social welfare policy, which is a care and concern for the neediest members of society. The major crossbar in the book that bridges the bitter polarities of the "Christian and National debate" on welfare policy and services is simple and spiritual: "how we might best respond to the *requirement* that we love our needy neighbors." On the surface, using a biblical mandate as the major building block for scholarly exploration in the policy and social sciences might seem trite and anti-intellectual. It is not so in this volume. Welfare policy has always teetered back and forth between how to turn into practice the everlasting care we are supposed to have for our neighbors while being firm at the same time. In some eras, our policies have been sensitive, and others have reflected the tough-love approach to helping the poor. Today we are strong on the tough and weak on the love.

This collection is important, scholarly, and meaty precisely because current welfare policy, cannot be understood or influenced without understanding what takes place at Main Street's busy intersection of religion, policy, and social service. Until the arrival of this work, many in the academic community, had whizzed through much of the vast activity at this busy but neglected scholarly crossroads. This omission has not only weakened our understanding of public religion, social policy, and social services but also has skewed our understanding of the entire nonprofit sector. As a result, the press has reported some interesting news on these matters, but the stories reflect good writing and good story telling, not always good analysis. And you can't blame the press—their stories are as good as their sources, so when few in the academy know what is happening on Main Street, it is hard to find a good source let alone the best one.

ANALYSIS OF POLITICS AND SOCIAL SERVICE LOCALLY: THE BIG PICTURE

The way we think about the poor in our communities and put services to help them into practice cannot be understood or influenced effectively without knowing what goes on at the busy intersection on Main Street. The Reagan era, current welfare reform, and the shifts in authority for design and delivery of social services, has had a huge impact on millions of people, tens of thousands of public social services programs, religious charities and congregations, self-help groups, and nonprofit agencies. Nevertheless, politicians, religious leaders, and scholars from conservative think tanks, without much stringent or independently reviewed research to back them up, have defined both the causes and remedies of welfare and other social service concerns. And the press has reported their findings.

Professor Theodore Hershberg (1989) noted somewhat harshly three distinct reasons as to why universities are not hospitable environments for research about applied public policy, and by extension social service, and religion:

(1) Public policy problems require interdisciplinary responses. But the social sciences in our universities are organized by departments and dominated by discipline-based research paradigms that make collaborative and interdisciplinary research exceedingly difficult. The resulting scholarship usually fails to provide adequate diagnosis or prescriptions for problems as they exist full blown in the real world.

(2) The audience for whom academics write is other academics—not practitioners or policy makers. Success is defined as a

response to one's scholarship, not efficacy in a real world application. The goal is not creating something that works, but publishing something that satisfies one's peers.

(3) The university environment is even less supportive when one
moves from public policy in general to state and local issues in
particular. Research done at universities is largely devoted to
issues at the national level. It demands greater resources and
enjoys far higher status than state or locally focused research.
The result is a dearth of locally-oriented research.

Because we have so few details about how the Reagan era budget cuts
actually affected local systems of public and private social services, we have
no base for analyzing how we should get through the next round of cuts.
Our lack of understanding clouds our perception of the ways religious congregations and charities offer social services and support public and private
nonprofit social agencies in their communities with volunteers, money, use
of their facilities, and other resources. Also troubling is that we do not have
a grasp of how sectarian agencies and congregations contribute to the
broader social welfare in communities by serving those not necessarily affiliated with their denominations or faiths.

Cuts in federal assistance in the 1980s and 1990s demanded that social
support had to be increasingly handled through the charitable efforts of
the religious community. Some might call this approach to policy an
unfunded mandate. *Without knowing know how the larger nonprofit and
public system of services operate in conjunction with the religious community,
it is quite difficult* to decipher *detailed aspects of social service in this country.* And that is exactly what we need now in communities large and
small—an analysis of the system of services that has gone through a transformation to increasing religious involvement. As the religious community is asked to do more, will its members, as their supporters claim, have
the capability, desire, and skills to handle increasingly complex social service roles tossed in their direction? Local systems do not do long-range
planning, and that will need to be done as they are asked to use their
resources in new and effective ways.

To do so, like it or not, communities will need academic assistance if for
no other reason than to help collect and analyze the base line information
so that people can develop new ways of helping based on coherent and

accurate information about the nature, scope, and resources to help solve, manage, and prevent local problems. The academic community skipped by the most dramatic shift in policy in more than half a century because it was not geared up to study local changes, even though much of the action took place locally. The question now *is how can the academic community become involved seriously in shaping the larger policy questions and assisting in finding practical solutions to bolster community planning efforts?* As I said in chapter 1, it will be difficult without an overarching analysis of the impact of the service contributions the people in these 300,000 congregations make, with their organizational arms reaching both inward to help their own members and outward to support sectarian and secular agencies in the nonprofit sector. Can regional, state, and local social policy be planned if it is not known how it is unfolding in various communities?

With no cogent analysis of this huge and complicated system of services, anybody who wants to take a shot at picking out one aspect of the prevailing flaws and turning it into the central interpretation of what is wrong with the system can do so without the fear of being challenged with grounded research and a tested analysis. Until the 1996 publication of *Welfare in America: Christian Perspectives on Policy in Crisis*, edited by Stanley W. Carlson-Thies and James W. Skillen, there had hardly been any organized thought, let alone sound research from the academic community, that might help the scholar, agency director, religious leader, or the concerned layperson figure out how to meet needs in local communities in a rapidly changing social service environment. We need many academic voices researching and debating at the national, state, and local levels the complicated intersection of politics, service, and religion.

OTHER RESEARCH

There were smatterings here and there, and even an attempt by the *Foundation News* in a September and October 1984 special edition that covered the religious underpinnings of philanthropy. In that special edition, noted nonprofit sector researcher Lester Salamon and colleague Fred Tietelbaum (1984) reported the findings of the first national study to explore the role of expanded religious involvement in service provision as a result of the Reagan budget cuts. They found that religious congregations increased their activities in providing direct services. They also found that congregations expanded their efforts at helping other service providers, and in addition religious congregations increased their financial support to religiously affiliated funding federations. For the most part their work on this subject ended there. Little mention was made in the 1980s about how the changes in federal policy were being felt by the agencies and organizations at the local level *as a community system of agencies and services with increasing religious involvement.*

The assumption that shrinking the public role in social services would stimulate religious involvement and more service development was correct, as I will demonstrate in later chapters. Nevertheless, as one might suspect, the major discussion of new local models of service delivery and their implications for social policy are still largely played out in the popular press, (Shapiro 1996; Klein 1997), foundation reports (Rainbow Research 1991), and books used by congregations to get involved locally (Peeler 1985), but not to a large degree in academic circles. In some instances (Cohen 1997; and Klein 1997), a romantic and pastoral analysis offers small religiously based programs as the life boats and ones we should take in redirecting our social policy and social services. But there is more to it than a spiritual lift.

Cutting public budgets again, as the new welfare reform has done in a major way, and expecting the religious community to absorb the strain on the system, is at best foggy policy. The system is huge and incomprehensible to those who do not know its workings. There is certainly no overarching analysis from politicians and the religious right that gives an important role to the religious community in the broader system of local services and few detailed local studies to clarify just whether the religious community, should, can, or will play that role successfully. On the surface, welfare reform is about job preparation and job placement. Public agencies will administer or broker that process. Beneath the surface, welfare reform is the hard-nosed, tough-love approach to ending poverty. But to accomplish the elimination of poverty, good policies need to focus on the constellation of factors that keep people in their jobs, and clearly there is not enough public money in the new welfare reform policies to accomplish such a goal nor was there ever any intention along those lines. We have the research on some of the things that work, but academicians do not partner up with local agencies for the long term and develop theory that informs and examines practice so as to further develop theory. We need that kind of approach.

Without a guiding framework, the religious community is expected to address voluntarily the other problems prohibiting people from climbing out of poverty. With no academic assistance to counter their analysis those on the religious and political right from the 1980s on have shaped the questions for diagnosing the flaws in the welfare system and offering how to fix them. The problems are often seen as simple and so are the answers. The cure to being idle and poor is a job and voluntary spiritual support if one is too weak to keep a job. Such an analysis does not reveal the complete picture of how to deal with issues at the local level. For a poor person seeking, finding, keeping, and growing in a job is intertwined with the availability of decent work, training, transportation, adequate housing, health of the individual and family members, and self- esteem. One needs understanding and the support her employer, family, and neighbors, not merely a job with no future. If a child is sick, or if a woman gets beaten up by her partner, spiritual help can be valuable, but that alone will not make local services handle the complicated problems of poverty effectively. There must be help from the academy to plan for these problems.

WHAT HAS BEEN THE FAITH COMMUNITY'S INVOLVEMENT?

The new policies assume that the faith community will assist in this transition from welfare to work. There has been little acknowledgment of its vast activity prior to this new policy, but we can reasonably say that they have been busy. The research of Hodkinson, Weitzman, and Kirsh (1988) was the first to shed light on the philanthropic efforts of the nation's religious congregations. Their work made enormous progress in outlining the national scope of congregational voluntary action in the United States and in mapping out the avenues for further investigation. Yet, that study was not designed to help clergy or human service planners better understand the congregation in the scheme of *community* social services. Other findings are displayed in figure 2.1, below..

FIGURE 2.1.

**Selected Findings from First National Study of
U.S. Congregations**

Conducted by Independent Sector

Individuals gave about $41.4 billion to 294,000 congregations of all denominations in 1986. Of that, $19.1 billion or 46 percent, was used by the churches and synagogues for non-religious programs including substantial donations to other organizations. Of the $8.4 billion given to other organizations, $5.5 billion went to denominational charities and organizations, $1.9 billion went to other charitable organizations and $1 billion was given in direct assistance to individuals.

Members of congregations donated $13.1 billion worth of volunteer time, about half of which went to non religious programs. Twelve percent, or $756 million, went to human service activities.

About 87 percent of congregations surveyed had one or more programs in human services and welfare including 80 percent in family counseling; 68 percent had programs in health; and over 90 percent of religious groups reported that their facilities were available to groups within the congregation. Six of 10 said their facilities were available to groups in the community.

Sixty percent of the congregations reported that they provided in-kind support like food, clothing, and housing to human service programs by outside groups (Hodkinson, Weitzman, and Kirsh 1988).

LOCAL RESPONSES

Some local responses to federal budget cuts in the 1980s were well documented (Magill 1986; Salamon and Teitelbaum, 1984; Salamon, Altschuler, and De Vita 1985; Salamon, Altschuler, and J. Myllyluomo 1990; Nathan, and Doolittle 1983, 1987). Clearly, the most interesting development in this funding shift was the reemergence of local religious institutions in providing for needy members of their communities. Yet, the analysis headed off in many directions describing how congregations were responding to the changes in policy, but paying little attention to the evolving role the religious community would assume in the constellation of local service provision by the 1990s.

McDonald (1984) found that many congregations gave grants to nontraditional or untested social programs. This became a common trend in the 1980s and 1990s, but my research, which I will explore in depth later, showed that grant-making by the religious community was not new; rather it increased dramatically and matured significantly. Case studies in the 1980s on increased congregational involvement focused on congregational activities in specific services like crisis intervention, welfare advocacy, and services to the elderly, and were a testimony to the fact that the local system of community social services needed buoying from the religious community. Congregations were in fact responding (Doll 1984; Negstead and Arnholt 1986; Wineburg and Wineburg 1986, 1987). Evidence mounted during the early and mid-eighties showing that private-sector involvement from the religious quarter was in fact taking shape. But research during that period was sparse, and it should be emphasized again *that studies usually did not tie increased activities of congregations to the operations of the broader service* system.

Below I show an exception. Table 2.1 shows the results of a 1988–89 study I conducted, charting the social services offered by 128 of Greensboro religious congregation. The eighth column to the right is important because it illustrates how many programs Greensboro's congregations offered after 1980 which was when the Reagan budget cuts started. The table also illustrates that the religious community had been offering an important system of services to their congregations *prior* to the cuts, and that a large increase in services took place after the Reagan cuts took hold. Food, clothing, and cash assistance programs ranked highest in new services offered. Half of the programs offered were for members of the broader community as well.

Table 2.2 shows the number of congregations, and the ways the religious community helped *Greensboro Urban Ministry*. This agency is exemplary in that as part of the Urban Ministry movement, it has garnered incredible interfaith support locally. It is a professional social service agency, and exemplifies what happened when the shift in policy went from government programs to local congregational initiatives. Greensboro Urban Ministry grew from a storefront operation in 1980, with six paid staff members, and volunteers representing less than 100 congregations, to a multi-service operation housed in a new $3.5 million facility, 59 paid staff members, more than 1,000 volunteers from more than 200 congregations, and close to a $2 million budget, much of which comes from local congregations.

The agency "spun off" its health clinic into a separate nonprofit organization called Health Serve Ministry, which is now housed in its own new facility next door to Greensboro Urban Ministry. Half of the members of the board of that agency consists of congregational representatives, the other half are from a local hospital that is using the clinic as an outpost to serve indigent clients and cut costs by using volunteer nurses, doctors, social workers, and others who come from local congregations. The outreach efforts of Greensboro's religious congregations to this agency show that congregations also reached out to community agencies extensively after the Reagan cuts. This point will be the entire focus of chapter 4, but here, I am able to show that this interfaith agency was growing in size because of the extensive support of the religious community. Seven of the nine programs listed (they will be highlighted by an asterisk) started after the Reagan cuts in 1981.

It might be noted when looking at table 2.2 that congregations were supplying much needed person power to the efforts of Greensboro Urban Ministry, and money and the use of their space as well. Greensboro Urban Ministry had its own facilities, so the sharing of space with congregations was not as extensive as other agencies that rely on the facilities of the religious community to accomplish all or part of their programming needs (see Chapter 4). The last column in table 2.2 is important in that it shows that congregations were collaborating to help Urban Ministry meet its program goals. Clearly, the evidence shows a dynamic and evolving relationship of congregations to its community's needs.

WHAT WE NEED FROM THE ACADEMIC COMMUNITY

I conclude this chapter with more about the role the academic community can play successfully in the new scheme of service delivery locally. Among the areas that need good research are: (1) understanding emerging and historical partnerships at the local level between the religious community and

Table 2.1

1988–89 Survey of Services Offered by 128 Greensboro Congregations

Service	Formal	Informal	For Members	Charge A Fee	For Community	Charge A Fee	Begun After 1980
Emergency Food Assistance	18	56	5	1	39	2	22
Clothing	20	40	7	2	30	2	15
Congregate Meals	8	6	9	2	6	2	2
Soup Kitchen	7	4	4	1	1	1	4
Emergency Shelter	3	11	2	2	2	2	2
Cash	30	31	12	0	27	0	10
Mobile Meals	22	8	1	0	9	0	8
Personal Counseling	27	37	17	0	25	0	7
Family Counseling	19	31	16	0	19	0	3
Phone Reassurance	11	21	12	0	11	0	5
Transportation	3	15	11	1	8	0	3
Housework for the Disabled	2	8	7	0	1	0	3
Housework for the Elderly	2	9	7	0	1	0	3
Home Health Assistance	4	3	2	0	2	1	1
Food Preparation	6	11	6	1	3	0	5
Legal Help	3	7	5	0	2	0	2
Help Finding Services	12	23	7	0	11	0	3
Child Care	16	4	4	2	8	6	3
After School Care	12	4	3	2	7	5	5

Adult Day Care	1	1	1	0	1	0	1
Tutoring	6	4	1	0	6	0	1
Employment Help	5	12	4	0	4	0	3
Pregnancy Counsel	7	8	4	0	5	0	1
Foster Care	3	1	0	0	2	0	2
Alcoholics Anonymous	23	3	2	0	10	2	3
Ala Teen	6	0	2	0	1	1	3
Narcotics Anonymous	8	0	0	0	3	0	3
Overeaters Anonymous	4	1	0	0	3	0	2
Mental Health	4	0	0	0	3	0	3

Table 2.2

1988–89 Survey of Outreach by Greensboro's Religious Community to Programs of Greensboro Urban Ministry

Service by Congregation	Providing Volunteers	Providing Money	Providing Goods	Providing Facilities	Collaborating With Others
Night Shelter*	22	37	28	0	8
Food Bank*	24	37	51	1	8
Soup Kitchen*	43	36	33	1	6
Clothing Room	19	24	49	1	7
Emergency Assistance	15	38	19	1	7
Project Independence*	17	20	8	1	8
Housing Rehabilitation*	15	17	8	1	4
Family Shelter*	14	20	15	0	2
Cheese Distribution*	10	8	1	1	4

*Program started after the Reagan cuts in 1981

social service providers; (2) learning more about the capacity of congregations and faith-based charities to handle more service responsibilities and building those capacities; (3) deciphering the process by which faith-based organizations choose to become involved in volunteering and providing other resources for community projects; (4) evaluating the effectiveness of involvement in community projects, for both the client, faith-based organizations, other members of the partnership, and the local community; (5) determining outcomes—whether the effort solved, managed, or prevented the problems designed to tackle; (6) understanding and delineating the roles and functions of faith-based congregations; (7) determining training requirements; (8) measuring costs of service and contributions of volunteers and other in-kind resources; (9) understanding how the interaction of these efforts noted above contribute to local policy development; (10) comparing different communities in order to develop new and testable policy theory. These and other areas were not examined during the time of the Reagan budget cuts and our policies reflect the dearth of understanding.

CHAPTER THREE

Budget Cuts or Buttercups

In 1982, when my son Zach was two years old, much of the conversation between my wife and myself was about the Reagan budget cuts. One day we were on a walk, and Zach said what I was sure was "budget cuts." To my dismay he was not interested in the politics of social services at age 2, rather he was pointing to the yellow buttercups the word for which my wife had taught him to say the previous day. To those who were affected, the budget cuts were not buttercups.

❐

SUMMARY

Four Major Points of Chapter 3

1. The human service system went through a largely unnoticed transformation in the 1980s.
2. Budget cuts stimulated much service activity but they did not make the system of services more efficient at service delivery.
3. The religious community, which had been a service provider, increased its activities in providing services on their premises, helping start new agencies, and supporting existing ones.
4. The policy of budget cuts may have caused some of the problems they were supposed to have solved.

❐

REAGAN CUTS AND EXPANSION OF COMMUNITY-
AND FAITH-BASED SERVICES IN GREENSBORO

The community human services system as we know it now changed as a result of the Reagan cuts. The Great Society programs of the 1960s, which followed the New Deal programs of the 1930s, clearly made local systems of services targets for criticism and policy change. The programs and services that resulted locally as a result of two eras of federal programs being cast on local communities, to some degree made, such systems top heavy, bureaucratic, and at some levels cold and impersonal. During the 1980s the Reagan policies consolidated a vast array of federal programs into block grants. Not only did communities see less money come into their the system of services locally, but they also had to face enormous challenges brought on by a combination of factors presented below that altered life for both the employees and volunteers in service delivery, and the people they served. Those challenges were unique in each community, but they had to be met in order to satisfy the urgent service needs of the eighties and the ones they were undoubtedly going to face into the 1990s. As we face a future of dealing with the demands brought on by reduced federal monies and programs, our leaders might keep in mind that the challenges of the previous era were not met with the success that budget cutters had hoped for. Reproduced in figure 3.1, below, is a 1983 statement from then Speaker of the United States House of Representatives Tip O'Neill highlighting the first round of the Reagan era cuts. The speaker's last paragraph was prophetic not in its political prophecy but in the consequences the cuts would have on the systems of services in communities nationwide.

FOUR CHALLENGES TO THE SYSTEM

Increased Responsibilities

The successful transition from the top heavy, bureaucratic, and supposedly impersonal system, to an administratively small, approachable, and accountable system called for in the Reagan years did not take place. While the system

FIGURE 3.1.

Statement of Speaker of the House of Representatives

Statement of Speaker Thomas P. O'Neill, Junior
August 25, 1983

At my request, the Congressional Budget Office has conducted a thorough analysis of President Reagan's budget cuts. The report contains some sad but timely information:

- On the issue of **fairness**—Despite repeated denials from President Reagan himself, Administrative cuts have been targeted to families of moderate and low incomes.

  Families with incomes under $20,000 have suffered cuts more than twice as severe as families in higher income brackets [**$415** as compared to **$175** in 1985]. **70%** of all Reagan cuts have been directed toward this income group.

- On the issue of **hunger**—Despite the President's recent statements, that he is "perplexed and concerned" at news of rising poverty and hunger in America, CBO documents that Reagan policies have contributed to it.

  Child nutrition programs have been cut by **28%**. A million lower-income children have been cut from the school feeding program.

- On the issue of economic **opportunity**—The president's record contradicts his recent political statements of concern for our country's disadvantaged citizens.

  He has cut job training programs **35 percent**; cut work incentives for welfare recipients **33 percent**; and has reinstituted the disincentives for able-bodied AFDC recipients to take jobs.

- On the issue of education—He has cut compensatory education programs for disadvantaged children by **17 percent** and guaranteed student loans by **27 percent**. Between 1981 and 1982, 700,000 fewer students received loans.

- Finally, on the issue of families—The President projects the image of a man concerned about the welfare of the average American family. His record shatters that image. He has denied millions of American families the basics of the American Dream.

  While non partisan in nature this report cuts through the smokescreen of Reagan public relations to the harsh truth of the Reagan record. That truth will have major consequences in 1984.

of the 1980s had been labeled as unresponsive, it had developed an internal consistency comprehensible to recipients as well as providers. Communities were expected to handle certain problems through their publicly financed mental health, public health, community action, and social service agencies. When they were unable to manage problems, they contracted with private agencies for support services. Such agencies—some independent and others under the United Way umbrella—had developed staffs and budgets partly because of the back-up and support roles they assumed in a community services network. Supplementing the public and private agencies were the service organizations, self-help groups, and churches.

Prior to the budget cuts of the Reagan era, many coordinated relationships between public and private agencies were contractual, founded on financial incentives. There were the informal ones that took place at the local level as a matter of course, as well as complex and intertwined sets of formal and informal relationships with the religious community that I will speak of in chapter 4 and later chapters as well. In Greensboro, North Carolina, for example, the mobile meals program was administered by a private agency and financed by a contract with the local department of social services. The decrease in social service block grant funds forced the canceling of the contract, eliminating the program (Wineburg 1984). Funds were restored through private sources, but the coordinating relationship in this service area was no longer strong and formal.

From January 1981 to July 1983, there was a 20 percent cut in federal funding for human resources programs (CBO 1983). It was expected that private agencies would expand their roles to compensate for service reductions. Many private agencies, however, lost public funding as well. I noted five in figure 3.2 below. Numerous contracts with public agencies and a large number of grants and programs such as the Comprehensive Employment and Training Act were eliminated. In 1982, a Campaign for Human Development survey found that 80 percent of private voluntary agencies experienced funding cutbacks, 46 percent lost staff, and 23 percent lost more than half of their paid staff.

Those reductions drastically curtailed agency capacities. With less money for their own programs and for contractual support, public agencies were forced to reduce optional services, eliminate support service contracts with private agencies like the mobile meals mentioned above, and economize across the board. Private agencies, because of fewer contracts with public

FIGURE 3.2.

Excerpts from the 11 page 1982 *Community Research External Appraisal* **document of the Greensboro Junior League.**
The League was monitoring the effects of the cuts locally.

The 1981–82 External Appraisal has focused on how federal, state and local budget cuts have affected and are expected to affect, services provided in Greensboro. It is obvious the elderly and the poor and their children have already felt the effects. In the past these groups have benefitted from a number of programs that Government has provided, all of which have been cut in some way . . . Additional information has been gathered from agencies dealing in human services.

EDUCATION

240.45 positions were eliminated these included: 147.2 certified teaching positions, 69 non teaching positions 24.25 cafeteria workers. Pay raises reduced, months of employment for some employees reduced. Title I reading and math labs eliminated. Funds for expansion items eliminated.

SOCIAL SERVICES

Two thousand people had food stamp allocations reduced, while 200 lost them altogether. Doctor visits and number of prescriptions for people on Medicaid were limited. An expected 21–22% reduction in Title XX funds with a corresponding reduction in services in day care, foster care for children and adults, adoption, counseling, child abuse prevention, Mobile Meals(eliminated completely as noted above) and a reduction in CHORE providers.

MENTAL HEALTH SERVICES

Eliminated 15 positions. Reduced in-patient services by 50%. Number of children with mental retardation receiving residential care cut by 1/3. Eliminated special adolescent care program sending those kids back to public schools. In service training funds reduced substantially.

THE SYSTEM

Five private non profit agencies under the 37 agency Umbrella of the Untied Way lost 1.06 million dollars. *United Daycare Services* closed 2 agencies, as shown below, and less federal money sought more revenue from the private sector— businesses, civic groups, foundations, individuals, and the religious community. In short, they were patching holes in a leaking vessel, the same one that policymakers said should have been casting the safety nets far and wide to help those who could no longer receive help from indifferent federal programs. Just at the time when their resources were in great demand, because the public agencies had taken such a huge hit, the private nonprofit agencies were faltering as well (Wineburg, Spakes, and Finn 1983).

The initial cuts of the Reagan years hampered the development of a new and more responsive local system in two important ways. Public agencies, the major service providers in a community services system, concentrated on providing services they had to by law. Their efforts increasingly focused inward on efficient management of operations to provide those services with fewer resources. This in itself was not drastic, but private agencies at the same time were seeking ways to survive. As the public agencies looked inward to cost-saving measures, private agencies ventured outward to find money and volunteers to stay afloat. Survival measures sometimes took precedence over comprehensive community planning efforts to solve, manage, or prevent local problems. Public agencies were forced to manage caseloads with less money, while private agencies divided their efforts between raising money and delivering services that were once in the public domain.

Growing Social Problems

Had the growth of social problems leveled off, community members might have been able to redevelop responsive service networks. That did not occur, however. Joanne F. Selinske, in the Summer 1983 *Public Welfare* reported that child protection services were reeling from cutbacks and noted that reports of child abuse had risen 89 percent from 1976 to 1980. In the same issue, Judith H. Cassetty and Ruth McRoy asserted that poor families headed by women would find it increasingly difficult to meet basic survival needs such as food, housing, and medical care. Little did they know how prophetic they were. The problems grew and the system of services to help were under great duress. Better education and prevention programs had to be let go by necessity.

The news article and the pictures shown in figure 3.3 note in a somewhat patronizing way the success after two previous unsuccessful attempts at the coordination of food distribution in Greensboro in the 1980s. The article and pictures point out the magnitude of the hunger in the Greensboro community and the early stages of what would increasingly become a wider connection between the public and private system of services, especially the religious community which I will explore below and in other chapters. In this case, Greensboro Urban Ministry, with its ever-increasing support from the religious community, really started its expansion in the early 1980s, as government funds were withdrawn (See figure 3.5, below). Providers faced hungry people, the task of wide-scale management of food distribution, and a host of other concerns that stretched the system of services. They faced increased drug and alcohol abuse, increased infant mortality rates, overcrowded jails, and the major new social and health problem of the 1980s—AIDS.

To maintain social stability, communities were required to confront these pressing problems and halt their growth. What critics of the welfare state fail to understand in their calls for more private initiative and increased religious support is that the cuts of the 1980s spurred more action than imagined. In a 1994 study of the riots following the not guilty verdict in the Rodney King trial in Los Angeles, researchers at The University of Southern California, in a larger discussion of the religious response to the riots that followed the Rodney King verdict, in a tone that is reflects disbelief, discuss the religious social service infrastructure in Los Angeles this way:

> The vastness of the social service infrastructure that has been created by the city's religious institutions rarely becomes visible. . . .
> The religious social service infrastructure has become vast, because

FIGURE 3.3

Recipients line up to receive food in public/congregation effort.

New distribution much improved

By MARK McDONALD
Staff Writer

The line was five and six deep in places, and it stretched for a couple of hundred yards down the driveway from the National Guard Armory, around the corner and up Franklin Boulevard for perhaps 300 yards.

Inside the cool, spacious armory, volunteers from the Greensboro Urban Ministry were packing 5-pound blocks of cheese, 4-pound boxes of dry milk, 3-pound containers of honey and 5-pound packages of flour into bags and boxes.

At 9 a.m., the distribution began with a special line for the handicapped and a new system worked out by the volunteers and the Guilford County Department of Social Services.

By late morning the lines were moving at a respectable pace; the recipients, especially those who recalled past food distributions, were appreciative of the new system.

"This is sure better than it used to be," said Charlie Shiver, 69, of 337 Gorrell St. "I got here about 6 a.m."

Compared to the distribution last August at the Urban Ministry's Asheboro Street facility, the giveaway started on greased runners. It was the sweltering heat, long lines and bitter complaints last year that led social services planners to move the distribution site to the Farmers Market on Yanceyville Street. But by last spring the program had grown so large that a new site was needed and DSS planners chose the armory.

People started lining up there as early as 4 a.m. today, and by 6 a.m. the line extended part way down the driveway, according to David Grantham, a county official.

Greensboro Police Officer R.A. Stone said the distribution created a "pitiful traffic situation" with cars lined up "as far as you could see up Market, down Bessemer and Franklin Boulevard." By 10:15 a.m., though, there were no traffic tie-ups.

And police officers also were quick to describe the crowd as polite and well-mannered. "They're being very cooperative," said Officer B.J. Bailiff.

Ralph Sheppard, a DSS administrator who oversees the program, said he was surprised by

Staff photos by Jim Stratford

(See Food, C3)

Bags of food line tables at National Guard Armory

Greensboro News and Record August 23, 1984. Reprinted with permission of *News and Record.*

the needs of the city have been vast, and because California's publicly supported infrastructure has been cutback in the face of the
state's tax revolt and of its long lasting recession. (Orr, Miller, Roof
and Melton 1994, p. 16)

That religious infrastructure, no doubt like the one in Greensboro and
communities nationwide, expanded during the 1980s. But they did it without ceremony.

The simultaneous rise in the volume of community problems and reduction in public funds did force public and private cooperation. But the unde-
sirable outcome of that merger was hastily conceived plans done in a crisis
environment, resulting in less than optimal services. Local human services
networks have always been limited in their technical capacity to conduct
comprehensive planning. But that became alarming when added to the
conditions of worker burnout brought about by growing responsibilities,
decreasing funds, and increasing social problems. This new but unorgan-
ized confederation of public and private agencies made the appropriate
planning and effective delivery of service difficult. In the 1980s and in part
today, a prevailing national mentality that cast the bureaucracy as the devil
and the private sector as the angels made it difficult to get a clear analysis of
who was doing what, and how it was being done locally. The result of this
mentality and the inattention by scholars made local systems of services
difficult to manage, and unable to conduct of comprehensive planning
operations.

Special Interest Groups

Maintaining service levels in the 1980s depended on the power of state and
local special interest groups and on the fiscal capacities of states and localities, according to Sara Rodenberry in the Winter 1983 *Journal of Urban
Affairs*. Welfare theorists Frances Fox-Piven and Richard A. Cloward (1983)
outlined various strategies for involving service professionals, students, and
clients in the electoral process. Local officials felt increasing pressure from
a host of emerging interest groups, each one calling for increased funds.
The Bay Area Advocates for Human Services in California was formed after
the Reagan cuts. One of its long-term goals was to "increase the ability to
lobby more effectively at both county and state levels for funding for all

human services," according to Stan Wisner in *Social Services Review* (June 1983). In Greensboro, North Carolina, a local group called Community Alternatives to Budget Cuts joined the Young Women's Christian Association, Junior League, and Parent Teacher Association to sponsor candidates' hearings focusing on human services issues. The information in figure 3.4 shows their plights and the emergence of an organization to find alternatives for people who were affected by a loss in services.

Efforts such as these proliferated as communities assumed greater service responsibilities. The groups that came together and acted in coalitions did not do comprehensive community social service planning. They did survival planning. In the situations where people could be hurt, the scurrying was to make sure people did not suffer. Other organizations, not in coalitions, often worked alone in maintaining or reconfiguring their links to support. The lobbying that was taking place was not necessarily in the interest of defining or refining comprehensive community welfare goals. It was defensive and tactical instead of proactive and strategic. This meant that groups with strong and carefully planned lobbying efforts, whether they took the form of well-organized pleas to county officials for more resources or quiet requests to churches for assistance, received more help. Those with equally important needs but less capacity to lobby received less assistance. I will demonstrate later that the religious community was a stabilizing and leveling factor in this reckless, dynamic, and competitive grab for help.

SEEKING PRIVATE SECTOR HELP

To compound those problems, few state and local governments replaced lost federal aid with their own money on a dollar-for-dollar basis, although both local city and county government in Greensboro increasingly funded private nonprofit agencies on a small scale. Over time, the community human services system became less comprehensive and more selective in the range of services offered and the type of clients served. As the examples in figure 3.4 above show, people were being hurt by the cuts and immediate responses were needed to help those people. More importantly, the catch-as-catch-can responses and the search for help to finance the new services

FIGURE 3.4.

1981 document from Greensboro's Community Alternatives to the Budget Cuts documenting how the cuts affected people.

Material supplied to the community alternatives to budget cuts task force, November-1981, to illustrate various problems related to loss of federal funds

MW, age 57, is on Social Security for his multiple disabilities. Prescribed for him are eight different medications for heart, muscle spasms, pain, stiffness, depression, arthritis and stomach upset, costing a total of $70 for a month's supply, or one-fourth of his income. Without public health, mental health and social services, and without these medications, he becomes aggressive, quits eating, gets stiff and might eventually die. Since the first of October, he has had to pay for his prescriptions. With rent, utilities, food and transportation to the doctor, he cannot afford them.

AM, age 42, was on Social Security for her handicaps. When the budget cuts came, her disability was scrutinized and since it does not fit into a category, she was cut from benefits. She has a seizure disorder, some retardation, and an extremely dependent personality, such that the Sheltered Workshop's most optimistic projection is that she might be able to keep up with long-term sheltered work, but she will never be competitive with her work.

SS, age 21, was in a college program and just a month from graduation. She had struggled to care for her child and go to school. Then day care for the children of college students was cut from the budget and she dropped out of school without a chance to finish in the foreseeable future.

MP, age 72, lives in a high-rise for the elderly and is not able to get out alone. She had a wonderful relationship with "her" social worker and homemaker who would keep her from depression and would take her out to pay bills, get groceries, and to obtain medical care. When her worker's office closed and her case was transferred to someone too busy to go see her and too unfamiliar for MP to trust, she felt abandoned and may at some time need to be placed in an expensive rest home.

KA, age 9, comes from a family with a great deal of conflict—verbal and some physical abuse. He is self-conscious about his appearance and ability because he is always put down for both at home. Although bright,

Figure 3.4, continued

he does not do well in school and has dealt with this by starting to lie and steal. He was in a program run by Social Services where he and a small group of others practiced reading, good relationships, positive self-image, and using community resources for problem-solving. KA blossomed and came to trust the group leaders as he had no other adults. He had one week's notice that the program was being cut due to funding cuts.

RB, age 66, lives with her daughter since she had been mentally disabled following a stroke. Her daughter would like to work but cannot leave her mother alone all day. Even when the daughter is there, she does not care for her mother's needs very well. When RB was going to adult day care, she enjoyed the interaction with others. The activities kept her active, and her daughter could feel that she was safe. Since the day care center closed because there were no funds to operate it, RB is at home with the danger of leaving burners on, of not taking her medicine, and of becoming increasingly disoriented as her daughter leaves for work each morning.

led to greater fragmentation. While collective strategies were needed to solve multiple community problems, increased responsibilities coupled with reduced funds contributed to the inability to effectively coordinate and plan for services on a wide scale.

When policymakers cut social programs, they often cause misery to people who go to bed innocently one night and wake up the next day demonized without services. That kind of policy process creates chaos and people get hurt. The consequence at the community level is that program development gets done in a constant state of emergency, which means that there is little chance for comprehensive community planning. During the Reagan era, agencies were in a state of stress and in relative isolation from each other because the independent pursuit of resources by different participants in the system of services created a competitive rather than a cooperative atmosphere.

It is true that public and private agencies worked together, as in the food distribution case shown above. It was awkward initially, but over time the awkward interconnections stabilized and developed a logic comprehensible to at least the "insiders." Nevertheless, this coherence in no way made the solving, managing, or preventing problems locally a smooth trip. The "new system of the 1980s" was really no better at preventing and managing human problems than the one it replaced, and may very well have been worse. While local initiatives were supposed to fill service gaps engendered by the federal budget cuts, those very cuts may have polarized local initiatives, and worse yet, they may have caused our inability to keep some problems from growing.

As has been mentioned earlier, religious communities have been involved in helping the poor long before the Reagan era. Table 3.2 below demonstrates this point and shows a more complete picture of congregational service provision at the sites of Greensboro's congregations and at the sites of community agencies during the Reagan era. Figure 3.5 shows the growth in just one faith based agency during the last twenty years. The next chapter will explore the intricate relationships between the religious community and social service community in much greater depth.

During the Reagan era and ever since, both public and private agencies, have increased their dependence on local congregations in Greensboro and elsewhere, and congregations have stepped up their service provision as well. In the case example of Greensboro Urban Ministry above, it is important not merely to see the growth of that faith based organization during two decades, but also to understand that its enlistment of the religious community as an essential service component created a large and complicated web of activities that changed both the way that agency structured its help to the poor and the way the rest of the community perceived the role of the faith community in social service provision. The growth reflected in Greensboro Urban Ministry meant a huge increase in activities in local congregations to supply the money, volunteers, food, and other resources that allowed this agency to grow. The broader local services system really was not becoming sleek and more efficient; it was responding to a combination of problems caused by the original cuts themselves, like increased hunger and homelessness, and new problems such as providing medical care and emergency assistance for indigent AIDS patients. Not only was the religious community active and mobilized to help in the growth of Greensboro Urban Ministry, the survey I conducted in 1988–89 of congregational involvement in other service activities (Summary in figure 3.6) also revealed that congregations were active in other agencies in the network of community social services as well. And besides reaching out, remember, they were providing services on their premises.

FIGURE 3.5.

Greensboro Urban Ministry's Growth. It began in 1968 as an ecumenical agency designed to fight poverty.

In 1980 Greensboro Urban Ministry, an interfaith agency, was supported by 90 congregations. There were a total of 100 different volunteers who recorded 10,260 volunteer hours of service. There were 6 full time paid staff members and an annual budget of $143,500. Today, Greensboro Urban Ministry has an annual budget of $1,537,000 and is supported by just over 225 congregations. It is housed in a new 3.5 million dollar building, the funds for which were raised by the community. It now has 48 full-time employees and 48 part-time employees. Volunteers logged 134,000 hours in 1999. It received 900,000 lbs of donated food in 1999, and just completed building 40, three-bedroom apartments for transitional housing, 32 efficiency apartments for single homeless adults, a child care facility, and new family shelter.

There are numerous other congregational and community based activities that don't get recorded in the annual figures. For example, the annual Crop Walk for the Hungry for Church World Service which raised $190,000 (one quarter of those funds remains local) and had 3,700 volunteers who averaged about 3 hours each on the walk. There is a night shelter for single adults, a shelter for families, a food bank, a soup kitchen, an emergency assistance program, a program that supports families make the transition from welfare to work, and a chaplaincy program, much like a hospital chaplaincy program. Since the 1980s, the agency has developed an intricately involved in-service coordination scheme with both public and private agencies. The new welfare reform will create the same chaos as the cuts of the 1980s.

One of the most interesting findings of that 1988–89 survey of Greensboro's congregations is that 18 percent of the services provided by the responding congregations (italicized above) came after the Reagan cuts, which characterizes their commitment to help build new ways of service. Just as startling is that 507 services were services offered by the congregations prior to the Reagan cuts (shown in table 2.1), which is a testimony to the long-standing involvement of the religious community in service delivery. Against the backdrop of the 1988 Independent Sector's national study

FIGURE 3.6.

Synopsis of major findings from my 1988–89 study of congregational involvement in human services in Greensboro, NC.

- 87 percent (or 111 of the 128) responding congregations provided volunteers or other in-kind support for one or more human service activity in the Greensboro community.

- Of the 128 responding congregations, 84% (or 107) offered at least one in-house service such as counseling, or transportation to appointments, telephone reassurance, and the like.

- In all, the responding congregations reported providing a total of 632, or about five formal and informal services per congregation.

- Of the 632 services, 125 or (18%) of those services were initiated after 1980.

- Of the 632 services, 248, or (39%) were offered to residents of the broader community. Exactly half or 64 congregations offer in-house programs to the community.

- In total, congregations were charging a fee for few services with child care being one of them.

- At the time of the survey, 85% of the 128 congregations had counseling services. Forty-one congregations provided those services through an established program, while sixty-eight congregations provided those counseling services on an informal basis.

- 40 or (31%) of the responding congregations housed Alcoholic Anonymous, Narcotics Anonymous, and/or Over eaters Anonymous programs.

- At the time of the survey in 1989–1990, 31% were involved in Hospice, helping the disabled, and or other home health care services.

- 57 or (44%) of the responding congregations worked with neighborhood groups.

- 104 or (81%) of the congregations said that they would participate in community-based programs in the future.

also noted in chapter 2, the findings in Greensboro were similar to the national findings on similar measures such as the average number of services offered by the congregations—about five per congregation in each study. While the religious community was rather quiet and unceremonious in its efforts to help, it had been delivering services to its members and neighbors for years. In addition, the religious community not only reached out into the service community to provide help for Greensboro Urban Ministry as the case example in figure 3.7 illustrates, they also increased their on-site service delivery by 18 percent in the Reagan years. Table 3.3 below shows how congregations helped other agencies too.

The combination of the cuts and the changing responsibilities left both the poor and the system of supporting services in a confused and weakened state. Nevertheless, congregations made the ideas behind the budget cuts of the 1980s legitimate. A possible reason why there were not more major outbursts in urban areas like Los Angeles was that the religious community stepped up its involvement in service provision, helped support existing agencies, and as table 3.2 (part of the larger survey discussed in the next chapter) shows, that the religious community in Greensboro helped develop new agencies as well. In some instances these new agencies were community development corporations designed to bring more financial aid into the religious community's service programs and at the same time solve community problems. The Welfare Reform Liaison Project that I mention in chapter 9 is a 1990s version of this type of organization.

Religious communities demonstrated that there was a capacity at the local level to fill service needs. With so much having been cut, the shock was in part absorbed by the religious community which simply did more where more was needed to be done. As table 3.2 above demonstrates, however, congregations in Greensboro had been initiating the formation of agencies since records were kept in 1917. What was new in the case of the growth of on-site services shown in table 3.3 and the growth of new agencies shown in table 3.2, was the pace of the growth. Interestingly, as table 3.3 demonstrates, agencies emerging from congregations range from both private, secular nonprofits, and religiously-affiliated nonprofits, to new governmental agencies.

Throughout different eras in our social service history, the religious community, was involved in the system of social services at the community level. Nevertheless as we call on the religious community to get more

FIGURE 3.7.

Excerpts from seven different written responses regarding congregational service taken from my 1988–89 survey of Greensboro's religious congregations.

Our congregation works with the needy who come to us for help with money, clothing, and food: street people, the sick and shut-ins, and elderly staying by themselves. We visit the elderly and carry them meals from time-to-time and pick up disabled people and carry them to church. We work this mission through our brotherhood and missionary clubs. We counsel by telephone, and pray for many people during their confinement to their home and hospital, including those not in my congregation.

We try to work with the community through various social services and by getting involved in the lives of those around us.

We provide as needs exist—sitters, finances, meals, financial counseling, etc.

We have worked with the neighborhood for many years—scouts, daycare, recreation, AA, community meetings, etc.—and constantly monitor and evaluate them.

We participate in our neighborhood crop walk and help those with clothing and food needs in our area as needed, if we have the financial resources

The pastor, church council, and board of finance evaluate the percent of giving which actually goes to work, rather than for operational expenses of any project. The congregation has the opportunity for any questions or comments in regard to outreach projects of the church. Special needs are made known . . . floods, sickness, etc.

We report the number of families given emergency food each month to the food banks we use and to the St. Vincent de Paul Society with whom we work.

Table 3.1.

1988–89 Survey of congregational outreach to other Greensboro Agencies
(By number of Congregations)

Agency	Volunteers	Providing		Facilities	Collaborating with Others
		Money	Goods		
Habitat For Humanity	41	29	7	3	11
Project Uplift*	9	10	3	2	2
Hospice*	31	24	6	2	7
Guilford Native American Association	4	5	7	0	2
South East Council on Crime and Delinquency*	2	2	0	0	0
United Services For Older Adults	13	11	3	1	5
Lutheran Family Services	16	12	10	6	5
Refugee Resettlement*					

*Started here in 1980 or later

Table 3.2

My 1992 Survey of Greensboro Agencies reveals that agencies that
developed out of congregational efforts increased dramatically
during the Reagan/Bush years.

Years	Agencies Formed
1917–1950	8
1951–1978	10
1982–1992	8

involved as we approach this next round of cuts, we lack a comprehensive
scholarly analysis of what the policy changes of the 1980s did to local service systems. The discourse is being shaped again by politicians and the
media.

First, I believe that the polices of budget cuts caused as much harm to the
people and the system of services than if nothing were done at all. Second,
the cuts to the system were healed in many ways by the religious community. Can the next round of cuts be absorbed by the religious community as
well as the last round? Does the religious community have the resources?
Perhaps the religious community is not able to handle the enormous service responsibilities of the welfare state, and so we need to look for ways of
studying and shaping better community partnerships. Otherwise, our
politicians will shape the next round of social policy, with little input from
scholarly research, much to the detriment of those who need help.

Table 3.3

Selection of Agencies Emerging from Congregational Action

Agency/Year Begun	Type	Service	Resources from Religious Community
Family Life Council, 1968	Private, United Way	Family Education	Volunteers, Money, Space
Pastoral Counseling Services, 1986	Private, United Methodist	Counseling	Money
Guilford Native American Association, 1976	Private, United Way	Urban Indian Center	Volunteers, Money, Space
Greensboro Youth Council, 1962	Public	Youth Leadership Training	Volunteers, Money, Space
United Services for Older Adults, 1977	Private, United Way	Multi-Service Center	Volunteers, Money, Space
Project Homestead, 1991	Private-Independent	Community Development	Volunteers, Money, Space

CHAPTER FOUR

If It Can't Be Counted It Doesn't Count

Throughout this book I will continue to illustrate the difference between the rhetoric of religious involvement in social services and the reality after nearly 20 years of research, trying to bring coherence to a discussion gone awry. One of the members of my community advisory group that helped guide the research that I will report in this chapter, Reverend Z. Holler, saw the research findings and characterized best what I want to say here: "Whenever people of faith put themselves in circumstances different from themselves, religion ceases to be talk and marvelous things happen." This chapter takes an accounting of those marvelous things.

⌐

SUMMARY

Major Points of Chapter 4

1. In this chapter I want to continue with a major theme of this work: social services and religion at the community level have had a longstanding and evolving relationship—each system influencing the other.
2. The policy debates about the capability, capacity, and desire for more service involvement from the religious community are not very realistic.

3. I will present findings here of a 1992–1995 study that illustrate that the relationships between the two systems are complex, intertwined, and evolving.

4. As such, we would do far better in policy and program development to study ways of refining the real partnerships that have evolved, sustaining the emerging ones, and creating conditions for the development of new partnerships that really work. It is damaging to push a political agenda without a clear understanding of what faith-based organizations can and cannot accomplish.

❏

An earlier version of this chapter appears in Ram Cnaan's book *The New Deal: Social Work and Religion in Partnership* (New York: Columbia University Press, 1999).

THE POLITICS OF RELIGION AND SOCIAL SERVICES

Marvin Olasky's book *The Tragedy of American Compassion* (1992) is the work most often cited for shaping much of the recent discussion of welfare reform policy and corresponding social service development. Olasky calls for a return to a pre-twentieth-century era of service design and delivery when people helped each other through their religious institutions with a spirit of piety, compassion, and an overarching emphasis on a type of charity *that avoided creating dependence.* As I noted in the Introduction, this thesis is especially popular among conservative intellectuals and politicians whose analysis of welfare and the system of services were influenced heavily by Gilder, Murray, and Mead, and reinforced by the policy approaches of the Reagan and Bush years. Some politicians, understandably eager to convince an exasperated public that they are finally attacking the causes of society's decay and government largess, have heightened their calls for more *involvement* from the religious community to solve local problems.

Politicians from both political parties have espoused the benefits of religious involvement in social services, and just 17 years after Ronald Reagan's 1982 story of the Good Samaritan, presidential candidates from both parties created campaign discourse that puts faith groups as keys to "civil society," as Democratic candidate Bill Bradley put it, as reported in *Time* magazine's article "Campaign 2000: Everybody's got Religion" (June 7, 1999, p. 58).The *Time* article goes on to briefly discuss each of five presidential candidates' views on the role of faith-based organizations in the provision of services. While one might infer from the article that this kind of talk is new, at least for Democrats, it's not. On the 1996 campaign stump, President Clinton spoke to the National Baptist Convention USA, which represents 33,000 primarily Black Baptist churches, urging the nation's churches to take the sting out of the tough new welfare bill by hiring people off the public rolls (Associated Press 1996). In a speech at Highland United Methodist Church in Raleigh, North Carolina Governor Jim Hunt, a Democrat, called on the religious community to "pitch in and make this happen." He was referring to the Work First program, which is North Carolina's welfare reform program (*Greensboro News and Record* 1996). The Republicans have had their say as well in increasing the ties between government and the faith community. Former Speaker of the House of Representatives Newt Gingrich, impressed by the volunteer spirit he found in the home building efforts of Habitat for Humanity, a Christian home building operation, supported legislation introduced by Representative Rick Lazio (R-NY) for a $50 million federal grant for Habitat and other organizations that build homes for the poor. Republican Governor Kirk Fordice of Mississippi proposed a program called *Faith In Families* (Edwards 1995), which encouraged each of the state's 5,500 churches and synagogues to adopt one of the state's 55,000 welfare families. While the state would continue its financial support for families receiving AFDC, congregations would provide practical and spiritual support through such an effort.

U.S. Senator John Ashcroft (R-Mo.) proposed the Charitable-Choice initiative, which helped smooth the way for religious communities to team up with social service providers. Approved in September 1995, as part of the Senate's welfare-reform bill and incorporated as section 104 of the The Personal Responsibility and Work Opportunity Reconciliation Act of 1996, it prohibits discrimination against a social service organization with regard to receiving federal, state, or local grants "on the basis that the organization has a religious character." This means that faith-based charities can contract with all levels of government—or receive funds in the form of vouchers or certificates—without having to change or suppress their religious identity. The legislation specifies that religious charities receiving government funds may require employees to "adhere to [their] religious tenets and teachings" and to submit to organizational rules "regarding the use of drugs or alcohol." Participating religious organizations would not be required to remove "religious art, icons, Scripture, or other symbols." Ashcroft's bill is now referred to as the "section 104" or the "Charitable Choice Provision" part of The Personal Responsibility and Omnibus Reconciliation Act of 1996. As a concession to those who fear a religious requirement for service, the measure also prohibits faith-based service organizations from discriminating against beneficiaries of their services "on the basis of religion, a religious belief, or refusal to actively participate in a religious practice." It specifies that no funds "provided directly to institutions or organizations to provide services . . . shall be expended for sectarian worship or instruction" (Frame 1995:65).

Senator Dan Coats (R-IN) likes to tell the story of the Gospel Mission, a drug-treatment center for homeless men not far from the nation's capitol. Under the leadership of John Woods, the mission successfully rehabilitates two-thirds of those who seek treatment there. Just three blocks away is a government-operated shelter with similar goals. But even though it spends 20 times more per person, that shelter boasts only a 10 percent success rate. Senator Coats has an explanation for the disparity: "The Gospel Mission succeeds because it provides more than a meal, more than a drug treatment. It is in the business of spreading the grace of God" (Frame 1995:65).

It may be more likely that Gospel Mission chooses its clients, or the clients self-select, therefore increasing the chance for success in Gospel Mission's programs. The government shelter, on the other hand, is probably more diverse. Comparing the success of a program that in some way selects its clients to one that has to select any client in need is not necessarily a good basis for policy development. Yet, like the story of the Good Samaritan used by President Reagan, Senator Coats without deeper analysis makes the comparison between the small religiously based service provider, and the large government financed program.

What Does This Mean?

Ending welfare as we know it is based on a somewhat misconstrued rationale. The thinking goes something like this: large-scale government programs that serve anybody and everybody are too large, too bumbling, and too bureaucratic to inspire those in need to help themselves. The major flaw in the design of large-scale government programs, besides being laden with huge costs, is that they, unlike the programs of their religious counterparts, do nothing to address the recipients' real problems. To those in agreement with Olasky, people become homeless, abuse drugs, and take up a life of crime because their fall from grace has induced a spiritual crisis that no quick fix, no government program, or no kindhearted social worker will ever heal. No government program can ever repair a broken spirit. Politicians inspired by Olasky's work would like to see public programs phased out over time (see table 4.1) in favor of a revival of private, especially religious, charity (Shapiro 1996).

Reagan/Bush Era vs. Clinton/Gingrich Era

Summoning local congregations and religious charities to deliver more of the nation's social services clearly follows the spirit of the Reagan and

Table 4.1.

Budget Cuts in 1996 Welfare Reform Law

Program	Cut/Increase from Current Law Estimates	Percent of Total Cut
Food Stamps	$23.3 billion	42.6
Supplemental Security Income	22.7 billion	41.7
Medicaid	4.1 billion	7.5
Child Nutrition	2.9 billion	5.2
Earned Income Tax Credit	3.5 billion	6.0
Social Service Block Grant	2.3 billion	4.5
Family Support	247 million	0.5
Social Security	85 million	0.2
Foster Care	232 million [increase]	0.5
Maternal child Health	253 million [increase]	0.6
Child Care	3.5 billion [increase]	6.4
Total	-54.5	100%

Bush social policies, captured in George Bush's now famous "Thousand Points of Light" campaign speech that simultaneously called for decreased governmental spending and increased local voluntary support for social welfare efforts. A March 8, 1990 request for new program proposals (*Federal Register*, 1990: 8555) stated the Reagan/Bush view clearly: **"Human service needs are best defined through institutions and organizations at the local level."** A major difference between now and then is that now there is a conscious attempt to target religious institutions *specifically* as the local organizations most suited to take the service baton from government.

WELFARE AS WE KNOW IT IS GONE BUT WHERE ARE WE?

We have been witnessing the first two stages in a cycle of reshaping and redeveloping the welfare state. The Reagan budget cuts and the Bush push for more nonprofit involvement locally has been followed by more budget cuts, targeting the religious community to step up its involvement in local service development. This second stage is supported by legislation like Representative Lazio's and Senator Ashcroft's, and by using political speeches to call for drawing more service from the religious community such as Governors Fordice and Hunt did in Mississippi and North Carolina, and President Clinton did on the campaign trail. Washington and some of the nation's statehouses never mention the already expanded involvement of congregations and religious charities in social service since 1981.

Mainline congregations and religious charities had stepped in locally and succeeded because their roots of service have wound around and through local public and secular service systems from the beginning of nationhood, forming interesting local partnerships and strong community bonds. On the other hand, the growing rhetoric, public influence, and political gains of the *religious right* in the 1990s created an atmosphere in which politicians began to announce that the religious community must step up its involvement. They did this without an overarching analysis of how the policy changes would affect the system of services locally. They ignored the fact that quite a bit of service activity has already happened throughout the 1980s and 1990s as a result of the efforts of the less vocal *mainline* religious community (Wineburg 1996).

Table 2.1 and the figures and tables in chapter 3 show the service activities of the congregations in Greensboro in the 1980s and demonstrate that congregations were involved in helping community agencies and giving service on site. Momentarily, I will present a summary of findings from a 1992–1995 study I conducted of Greensboro social service agencies to look at four issues:

- What are the relationships between the religious and social services communities regarding solicitation and use of volunteers, facilities, and money?
- How do the relationships form?
- Can any of the changes in the relationships be attributed to the Reagan/Bush policies?
- Are there discernible patterns in the relationships that may be similar in other communities?

When this data is set against the backdrop of the early work of Salamon and Tietelbaum (1984) which demonstrated that congregations nationally were involved in responding to the Reagan cuts; the work of Hodgkinson, Weitzman, and Kirsh (1988) which charted the vast community service activities of the country's religious congregations; the work of Orr, Miller, Roof, and Melton (1994) who outlined the vast religious infrastructure of Los Angeles; and most importantly, the recent research from Cnaan's (1997) six-city study of the community service activity of congregations housed in historic religious buildings, documenting in fine detail the extensive community and on-site activities of congregants in Philadelphia, New York, Chicago, San Francisco/Oakland, Indianapolis, and Mobile, there is no other conclusion to be drawn than the following: The amount of social service activity emerging from the religious community has been vastly understated. As such, its capability to respond to another round of public budget cuts (see table 4.1 above) has been misrepresented in the political realm.

The results of my study challenge the prevailing notions of how the social service sector actually operates with regard to its interconnectedness to the religious community. What follows is a look at the interconnectedness between one town's religious community and its social service community. On one level it is a description of the religious community's contribution of volunteers, money, and their facilities to both public and private nonprofit agencies in the Greensboro community. The findings reveal a dynamism that neither scholars on the left nor right have made part of the public discussion of religion, social service, or the larger talk of civil society. When we look deeply at the complex interactions among people and local institutions that the findings represent, what is left is the glue of civil society, people, and institutions showing care, concern, and commitment over the long haul. The glue holds things together but is resilient enough to allow the people and institutions to expand, adjust, reshape, and respond to changing conditions over time. The glue that I will describe is what gives each community its distinct character and allows it to share a common culture with other communities. No analysis of the social service dimension of the nonprofit sector and religion can ignore this interaction. The following summary outlines the results for phase one of the 1992–1995 study which was to survey local agency directors in Greensboro, North Carolina, to determine how their agencies use volunteers, money, and facilities of local religious congregations.[1] The second phase examined six agencies in depth to see closely the inner workings of the congregational-agency relationships.

GENERAL VOLUNTEER USAGE BY
GREENSBORO AGENCIES

It would be helpful to provide a general backdrop of volunteer use by the local agencies to make clearer just how enmeshed the religious community actually is with the broader helping efforts in Greensboro. Figure 4.1 is a synopsis of the agencies and their functions in the community.[1] In all, 78 percent of Greensboro's agencies use volunteers. Half of the agencies use more than forty-five volunteers in various ways, while half of the agencies use less. The chart below, Figure 4.2, shows agency use of volunteers who serve on behalf of their congregation. Agencies like the Boy Scouts, Girl Scouts and Red Cross use more than one thousand volunteers, many of whom do so as congregational representatives. About 16 percent of the responding agencies calculate the dollar amount of their volunteer services. Eleven percent (16) of the responding agencies reported an estimated dollar figure for volunteer usage which totaled $1,554,000. Half of the agencies claimed above $45,000 in volunteer contributions. Another 12 percent (18) agencies who do not regularly calculate the dollar amount of volunteer services but did for this questionnaire, estimated $3.8 million in support. Only a small number of agencies calculated the financial worth of their volunteers' service from congregations. This is a very time-consuming and resource-consuming task and one that most agencies do not do. Neverthe-

---

[1] *Research Procedure*: I surveyed 193 public and private social agencies and self-help groups listed in The United Way's Directory of Greensboro's Agencies. Greensboro is a mid-sized Southern community of 190,000 people located in a metropolitan area of close to one million people. One hundred and forty-seven agencies responded to the mail survey. There were two rounds of follow-up phone reminders to respondents, which increased the initial 42 percent response to 76 percent. The statistical margin of error is plus or minus 3 points.

less, Greensboro Urban Ministry (see figure 3.7), documented 60,000 hours of volunteer service in 1992. At $5.35 an hour that is a contribution of more than $300,000 in volunteer labor from the religious community. Considering that Greensboro Urban Ministry and other agencies have doctors, lawyers, accountants, and other professionals donating their time, the $300,000 figure is conservative.

Congregational Volunteer Support

Looking at that same picture of the community's volunteer effort focusing on the religious community's contribution to the overall volunteer support of local agencies, sixty responding agency directors (49%) claimed that some of their volunteers serve as representatives of their religious congregations. On the surface, understanding this relationship is simple—congregations help out considerably. Underneath the surface things get blurry. Out of the 51 percent of the agency directors who answered that they did *not* use volunteers from religious congregations, 39 percent of them explained that they use volunteers who belong to religious congregations, but they also indicated that the volunteers did not serve as representatives of their congregations. This finding suggests that the glue of care and concern for others works *formally* and *informally* to seal the connections between the religious and social service communities. Such bonds have an evolving quality to them. Seventeen percent of the agency directors reported that they were interested in congregational volunteers, but that they had not yet developed congregational contacts.

Agency Use of Congregational Volunteers

The graph in figure 4.2 shows a portrait of the interdependent nature of the relationship between the religious and social service community. Fifty-four percent of the agencies who use congregational volunteers, use between one and twenty-five congregational volunteers at their agencies. Fifteen percent use between twenty-six and fifty congregational volunteers, and thirty-one percent use over fifty congregational volunteers. Using volunteers for direct services, which includes activities such as counseling, transporting people to various appointments and places, and directing groups, was ranked by 43 percent of the agencies as being the most frequent activity performed by congregational volunteers. Twenty percent of the agencies used congregational

---

FIGURE 4.1.

Agency Functions

Profile of Responding Agencies. Twenty-eight percent of the responding agencies classified themselves as public agencies, while 72% of the agencies labeled themselves private agencies. A further breakdown shows that close to 9% of the responding agencies classified themselves as religiously affiliated, 14% of the agencies claimed a United Way affiliation, 20% claimed to be independent agencies (non United Way, nor public), and 14% were categorized as self-help organizations. Thirty-six percent of the responding agencies were affiliated with national agencies. Thirty-one percent of the organizations had yearly budgets of less than $100,000. Forty percent had budgets between $100,000 and $1,000,000. Thirty percent of the responding agencies had budgets of over $1,000,000.

The major services offered included: Community Education 50%, Individual Counseling 44%, Information and Referral 42%, Family Counseling 36%, Youth Counseling 25%, Service to the Elderly 15%, Substance Abuse Counseling 14%, Financial Counseling 13%, Telephone Counseling 12%. Thirty-eight percent of the agencies employed between 1 and 4 full-time employees. Thirty-five percent of the agencies employed between 5 and 20 employees, while 26% of the agencies employed more 20 full time people. Fifty-two percent of the responding agencies employed between 1 and 4 part time workers. Thirty-two percent employed between 5 and 20 part time employees while 16 percent of the responding agencies employed more than 20 part-time employees.

---

volunteers most often for administrative purposes, which included planning, fund-raising, or board member participation. Five percent of the agencies used congregational volunteers most often for secretarial jobs, and three percent used congregational volunteers most often for custodial services.

The findings here indicate that congregational volunteers are and have been extremely important to the operations of Greensboro's social service agencies. The agencies used various methods of recruiting volunteers ranging from newsletters to old-fashioned personal contacts. The agency-congregational volunteer link appears dependent on an agency employee who is also a congregation member using personal contacts to broker the relationship between his or her congregation and the agency. These findings, combined

FIGURE 4.2

Agency Use of Volunteers from Religious Congregations

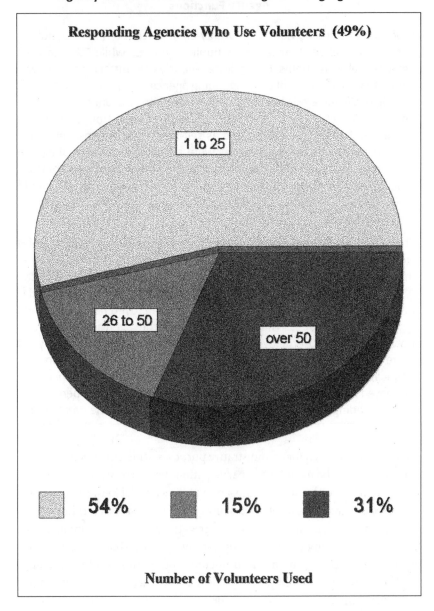

with the breakdown of full- and part-time employees noted above in table 4.1 above, demonstrate clearly that a substantial portion of Greensboro's agencies and social service organizations rely heavily on part-time employees and volunteer labor. Much of this support comes from religious congregations.

Eleven agencies in Greensboro were using more than one hundred volunteers from religious congregations at the time of the survey. Those eleven agencies included The Red Cross, Girl Scouts, Greensboro Jewish Federation, Greensboro Crisis Pregnancy Center, Shepherd's Center of Greensboro, Greensboro Youth Council, Greensboro Urban Ministry, Boy Scouts, Lutheran Family Services, Voluntary Action Center, and AGAPE. It is certain that close to 10 percent of the agencies, representing public (Greensboro Youth Council) and private nonprofit (The Red Cross) in the Greensboro community are quite large and have been dependent on the religious community for its pool of volunteers. Will the next round of cuts or the demands made by the new welfare reform strain this set of interrelationships? What is important to understand is that such partnerships are voluntary and stabilize a community. Politicians who think that the religious community or voluntary sector has unlimited resources and continue to pressure it to do more without providing ways to nurture and sustain the prevailing partnerships, risk damaging these partnerships.

Agencies attempt to keep labor costs at a minimum while trying to accomplish their missions with the maximum human and spiritual touch. Congregations reach out to make sure that they make a difference. It is fair to say that even though the system of services is already quite resourceful, it will have even more pressure on it to respond as it braces for the next round of cuts to take hold. I do not believe that it has the capacity to respond as effectively as it did with the cuts in the 1980s. I believe it is safe to conclude that congregations are contributing greatly to reducing the labor costs of local agencies through volunteers, and that their offerings don't make up much of the analysis when we talk about the contributions of the religious community to the social services and nonprofit sector.

Length of Volunteer Use

Figure 4.3 shows that 58 percent of the agencies who used congregational volunteers had been doing so for more than ten years at the time of the survey. This means that they started doing so before the Reagan budget cuts of

FIGURE 4.3

Number of Years Agencies Were Using Volunteers from Religious Congregations in Greensboro at the Time of the 1992 Survey

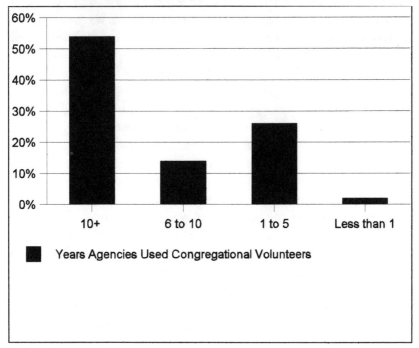

the 1980s took hold. Forty-two percent started using volunteers in the Reagan years. Fourteen percent had been using them for between six to ten years, and twenty-six percent had been working with volunteers from local congregations for one to five years. Two percent had begun using these volunteers in the year of the survey.

SEEKING AND RECEIVING FINANCIAL ASSISTANCE

As the policies of this newest era take hold in localities we will hear congregations being called on to give money as well as volunteers to support programs. Nevertheless, the findings from this research project conducted in the early and mid-1990s show that congregations give money as well as volunteers. Forty percent of the agencies sought financial support from local religious congregations. Thirty percent were receiving financial support from congregations at the time of the survey, while twenty-two percent were not receiving funds at the time of the survey but had received congregational finances in the past.

Only forty-eight of the responding agencies had never received funds from religious congregations. In addition, twelve percent of the responding agencies did not seek money from congregations but had received funds anyway. Although the public agencies experienced strong criticism during the Reagan years, it is suprising to find public agencies receiving funds from the religious community. Yet the respondent from the Public Health department wrote a note on the questionnaire indicating that while the Public Health Department did not get funds directly from congregations, the prenatal unit had an *Adopt a Mom* program, where a local congregation adopted a pregnant mom who could not afford prenatal care and "paid her prenatal cost and transportation costs." The respondent also noted that she and a member of her staff brokered the relationships with the congregations. In the introduction of this book I noted that the theoretical ideas of residual and institutional services were interconnected at the local level. This is an example.

Figure 4.4 illustrates the evolving nature of the relationships between the religious and social service community. The first column shows that 52 percent of the agencies in Greensboro received money from the religious community. The second column just shows that 48 percent of the agencies in the study did not receive funds. The third column shows that 31 percent of the agencies had been receiving financial assistance for more than ten years prior to the survey and therefore began doing so prior to the Reagan years. The fourth column illustrates that 69 percent of those agencies that had received congregational finances, *started receiving them in the Reagan era.* Not only did the religious community step up its giving of volunteers in the Reagan era, but it also gave money to nonprofit organizations as well. This finding suggests that congregations and agencies were forming more than simple, ad hoc, incremental relationships. They instead were forging deep institutional relationships, something overlooked in the call from Olasky to move our welfare state services back to the religious community. Two elements that constitute the glue that seals the social service and religious community are the spirit of volunteering and giving money.

FIGURE 4.4

Number of Agencies Receiving Money or not Receiving Money, from Congregations.

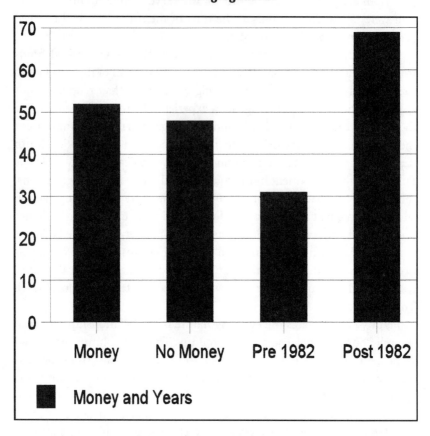

Note: Budget cuts really did not kick in with full force until 1982, so I am using that date to divide the pre- from the post-budget cut era.

SEEKING THE USE OF CONGREGATIONAL FACILITIES

Volunteers and money are not the only important congregational resources used by community agencies; so are the facilities. Sixty-six percent had used facilities of local religious congregations and thirty-four percent had never used them. The breakdown of the way agencies used congregational facilities looks like this: 36 percent were using congregational facilities at the time of the research, and 30 percent were not, but had used them in the past, so that a total of 66 percent of the community's agencies had been using congregations at one time or another. Of the 36 percent of the agencies using facilities at the time of the research, almost three quarters of them (73%) did not pay rent. Of the 27 percent who did pay rent, seven out of ten of them paid a reduced rate. Only about 6 percent of the agencies that used facilities paid a fair market rental rate. This finding shows clearly that congregations are benevolent and are open to allowing agencies to use their facilities at reduced rates or usually no rent at all.

Uses of Congregational Facilities. Twenty-six percent of the agencies use the church or synagogue facilities for educational purposes, 17 percent use them for agency meetings or retreats, 11 percent use congregational facilities for community meetings, 7 percent use them for services for the developmental disabled, blind, or elderly, and 7 percent use facilities for their offices. Given that community education is an important service function of agencies as noted above, it is clear that congregations serve as community education centers. Forty-six percent of the responding agencies have been using religious facilities for less than ten years, and fifty-four percent for more than ten years. This finding indicates that agencies are using congregational facilities so they can have the space necessary to accomplish their missions. It also suggests that a substantial use of congregational facilities took place after the Reagan budget cuts took hold. Congregational facilities serve as homes of some secular agencies. Some agencies are operating programs out of congregational facilities. Others are conducting community education projects or holding yearly meetings there. They are using the facilities on a daily, weekly, monthly, and yearly basis. Agencies are accomplishing different aspects of their programming by using congregational facilities.

Frequency of Use

Fifteen percent of the responding agencies use the congregational facilities everyday, twelve percent use facilities once or twice a week, twenty-one percent use them once or twice a month, and fifty-two percent use them once or twice a year (figure 4.5).

Other Types Of Support

The responding agencies noted a list of other contributions from Greensboro's congregations. Fifty percent of the agencies acknowledged receiving food, forty percent transportation, twenty percent free copying, twenty percent donated goods like baby supplies, and seventeen percent noted the free use of the congregational telephone. All-in-all congregations have been and still are helping agencies in many supporting roles besides providing them volunteers, money, and space.

GREENSBORO IN THE REAGAN/BUSH YEARS

What is first important to recognize is that eighteen percent of Greensboro's social agencies were started by congregational initiatives. The development of these relationships had been ongoing. Proving conclusively that the Reagan/Bush policies caused increased congregational efforts in Greensboro is clearly secondary to understanding what happened to congregational involvement in the 1982–1992 period when the Reagan/Bush retrenchment policies prevailed. What happened is clear. The data show several interesting trends. In any 10-year period from 1917 to 1992, the creation of new agencies increased no more than 10 percent with two exceptions. From 1968 to 1978, there was a 16 percent growth. In the 1982–1992, period there was a 26 percent growth in the creation of new agencies. It appears that new agencies started more rapidly in this era than others.

From 1982 to 1992, 27 percent of all congregational initiated agencies came into being. This was the highest percentage of any 10-year period. One thing is certain. During the Reagan/Bush era, both agency development and congregationally spawned agency development increased dramatically, and the interactions between the two communities changed from an incremental to a more comprehensive relationship as well.

Ram Cnaan's study of congregations in Philadelphia also found that the nonprofit groups emerged from Philadelphia's historic religious congregations (Cnaan 1997). As in Greensboro, it has been extensive. On average Cnaan found that almost 38 percent of the congregations he studied spun off about two programs or organizations. The one exception was the

FIGURE 4.5.

This Figure Demonstrates that Agencies Use Congregrational Facilities on a Regular Basis

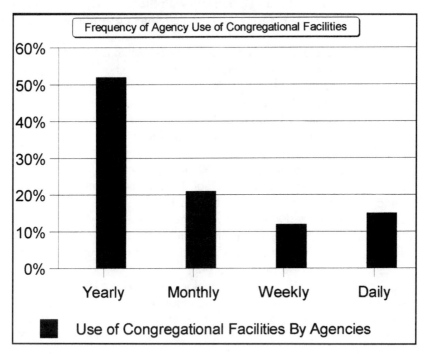

Frequency of Agency Use of Congregational Facilities

Use of Congregational Facilities By Agencies

Arch Street Friends Meeting House which over its long history had 140 community-based organizations spin off from it premises. If congregations and agencies continue to forge new relationships based in part on the multiple use of resources, congregations will have a much greater impact in the distribution of resources within the service network than ever imagined.

What do these relationships mean in Greensboro?

There is a deep and intertwined set of relationships between the social service and religious communities that developed over time. (See figure 4.6.) Congregations have been and still are providing volunteers, giving money,

FIGURE 4.6.

An Example of How Relationships Develop:
Origin of the Relationship with Black Child
Development Institute and the Religious Community

Me: Was Black Child Development Institute established directly as a conduit for congregational resources, did it start in a church—how did it really get going?

You probably should have asked Sarah Herban who was the founder. Sarah is a part of Bethel AME Church and has been for a long time, and as you know Sarah Herban was also co-founder of the National Black Child Care Development Institute.

Back in 1970 she was sent by the Women's Educational Equity Act to go throughout the South and take a look at women and women's issues to find out what impacted women the most.

What she found is that women were most concerned with their children, issues of immunization, proper child care, education, and things of that nature. So she went back to Washington and said the best thing we could do would be to found an organization that would focus on Afro-American children, and that therefore the Black Child Care Development Institute on a national level was founded.

Interestingly enough, Marian Wright Edelman was her intern at the time, they went throughout the Southern states. When she came back to Greensboro in 1978, she went to the churches and the congregations to begin to take a look at establishing an affiliate of the national here in Greensboro and because of her own strong commitment and her own involvement in the church that is where she began. The first members for Black Child Development Institute came not only from her family members who were all members of the congregation, but from the congregation itself.

Our early meetings in the beginning were held at the church, but we had no office and no established network, everything came through the utilization of the church facility and a congregation of volunteers. I think that throughout the years what has happened since my involvement, since about 1987, has been to see how the church has supported not only the Institute itself but the programs of the Institute.

We have one site at Bethel AME Church which has been there for five years and we are there twice a week, every week. We had a site out at

---

Figure 4.6, continued

Friends Home in the retirement community itself. As you know at the present time we have 13 tutorial sites; we have one site in the Laughlin Memorial United Methodist Church where we get free services in terms of space utilization, etc. for the tutorial program, but also the church is the spot where our black child choir practices and auditions and that is on a bi-weekly basis. So there is a lot of activity in the church as it pertains to the Institute itself.

Child Development Institute did a prayer breakfast for children and we have conducted that for several years running, where we would go right to the ministers and talk about issues that impacted children and how best we could work with their congregation in getting volunteers to become involved with children and children's issues. We go to the Pulpit Forum and naturally when we start fund raising, we go directly to the churches too.

---

and offering the use of their facilities to local Greensboro agencies. To reiterate a point made earlier, close to half of the agencies surveyed used congregational volunteers, 52 percent have received congregational money, and more than 65 percent have used the facilities of congregations. The relationships go far beyond the mere solicitation, distribution, and receiving of goods and services, however. *Religious congregations, in many cases, are an integral part of agency operations, providing thousands of volunteers, money, and buildings.*

This exchange goes both ways. The local agencies serve as conduits, or as the organizational literature has called them, mediating structures (Berger and Neuhaus 1977) between the charitable impulses of members of religious institutions and the people they want to help. The notion is also important, because when we have been asked to think systemically about what holds civil society and community together, the answer, from de Tocqueville on, has been voluntary associations and the religious institution. Greensboro's congregations are spawning new agency development and have done so continuously since 1917. The Cnaan (1997) study found this phenomenon on a national scale as well. Figure 4.6 shows a slice of the Greensboro story.

Today, congregations do not necessarily have to start an agency to display their care and concern. Existing agencies are providing numerous opportunities to help, and congregations, as the information provided here and elsewhere shows, are responding generously. Nevertheless by stimulating agency development, congregations have spun themselves into the web of the social service network to the degree that there is a surprisingly strong interdependence. Agencies are very pragmatic, especially in the use of congregational resources. The substantial use of congregational volunteers, money, and facilities from multiple congregations, and an extensive use of part-time employees, illustrates clearly that many of Greensboro's agencies and social service organizations are already intertwined with the religious congregations to the point that a blanket summons for the religious community to help in welfare reform seems unrealistic. With the continual stress for agencies to use charitable contributions in efficient and effective ways, one wonders if other communities could learn better methods of collaboration by studying the strong efforts by the religious and social service communities in those cities that have documented the efforts.

Clearly, one of the more noteworthy findings of this study is the relationship between an agency's use of a congregation's facility and its obtaining other resources. The data shows an evolutionary pattern developing toward a more comprehensive set of agency and congregational relationships. It seems that when a congregation offers its facilities to a community social agency, it is actually offering the community a special membership into its broader spiritual life, and thus acknowledges its own institutional commitment to the broader community.

Underneath the facts, figures, descriptions, and accounts in this chapter, is a picture of a community's spirit. While I don't believe that we have developed the measurement tools to completely assess a community's spirit, I do believe that we can sketch in some detail a picture of a community's everyday effort to turn its inner convictions regarding caring for its neighbor into outward form. I hope what has emerged here is a clearer picture than the one we had before, one I hope will stimulate a new set of questions for demographers who study American religion and nonprofit agencies, and for scholars and practitioners as well. Any analysis of either set of institutions without considering the profound partnerships discussed here, is incomplete.

APPENDIX
OTHER MATTERS IN CONGREGATIONAL SUPPORT

Volunteers

Methods of Volunteer Involvement. Fifty-three percent of the agencies using congregational support indicated that they had an organized method of involving volunteers from congregations, while 98 percent explained that they did not train volunteers from congregations differently from other volunteers. Just over half of the responding agencies reported that an agency staff member brokers the relationship when seeking congregational volunteers. Thirty-one percent responded that board members broker the relationship, and six percent answered that a volunteer brokers the relationship.

Denominational Volunteering. Just over half of the agencies who used congregational volunteers estimated the number of congregations supporting them with volunteers. Of those agencies, 38 percent used up to five different congregations for volunteer support, 24 percent used between eight and ten different congregations, while 14 percent of the agencies used up to twenty different congregations and 21 percent used twenty five or more different congregations for volunteer support. Once again, these findings, and the one above, demonstrate that congregational volunteering was on the rise in the early 1990s and that agencies sought and obtained volunteers from multiple congregations. Again such findings raise the question as to what are the real limits of the community's congregational capacity to give. How will the religious community handle increased demands?

Approaches to Congregations. Forty-one percent of the responding agencies indicated that most often the spiritual leader of the congregation was the chief contact person, thirty-three percent noted that a community leader was the chief contact, twenty percent cited a member of the agency who was also a church member, and seven percent reported that a volunteer or church staff member was the chief contact. When asked to rank the key elements in brokering the volunteer relationships, personal contacts and the reputation and track record of commitment of the congregation were highest, at seventy-eight percent each. Fifty-four percent of the agencies send newsletters to congregations announcing volunteer opportunities at their agency, and seventy percent of the agencies have additional ways of forming volunteer relationships with local congregations like a speakers' bureau or working through the local Voluntary Action Center. This clearly suggests that the agencies rely on a two-pronged process of resource development from the religious community that requires both the development of individual relationships and the nurturing and sustaining institutional bonds.

Money

Multiple Congregational Financial Donors. Forty-eight percent (29 of the 61) of the agencies that have received funds received it from between two and ten different congregations. Thirteen percent of the agencies involved up to thirty different congregations. Eight percent of the agencies received financial support from between thirty-eight and one hundred different congregations. This finding suggests that agencies are using congregations as mini-grant making sources in that they are seeking and receiving funds from multiple congregations.

Black, White, and Asian Giving of Money. Thirty-six percent of the responding agencies have received finances from Black congregations, sixty-four percent from received funds from white congregations, and two of the agencies had received funds from Asian and Hispanic congregations. There seems to be a greater number of agencies soliciting and receiving funds from white congregations than from Black congregations. Much more research needs to be done to understand the significance of this finding. It may be that the 64%–36% ratio reflects the racial make-up of local agencies staff and board. Much of the solicitation for funds is done by board members and staff of agencies who are congregational members, and they are mainly white. Greensboro's Black population is close to 30 percent, so it is plausible that this finding was a reflection of white and Black staff and board members going to their own congregations for funds. It may be that white congregations were perceived to be wealthier than Black congregations and thus were solicited more often.

Solicitation Approaches for Money. Forty-seven percent of the responding agencies use board members to broker the financial arrangement.

Thirty-nine percent of the responding agencies use a member of their staff to broker the financial relationship with congregations. Forty-three percent of the responding directors said that they broker the financial arrangements with congregations. Forty-five percent of the agencies indicated that the spiritual leader of the congregation was the chief contact person when seeking financial contributions, twenty-six percent responded that a community leader who is also a member of the congregation was the chief financial contact person. Twenty-two percent noted a member of the agency who was also a church member as the contact person.

Thirty percent of the responding agencies reported that they request money through annual solicitations to all congregations in the local community, thirty-one percent use informal requests to selected members of a select group of congregations, thirty-three percent send informal requests to a specific person from a select group of congregations, and twenty-six percent percent send formal proposals to selected members from selected congregations. Twenty-nine percent of the agencies noted that they did not request congregational finances. Instead they were approached by the congregations.

Space

Black, White and Asian Facilities Support. Twenty-eight percent of the agencies receive facility support from Black congregations, while fifty-two percent receive facility support from White congregations. Two percent are receiving support from Asian and Hispanic congregations.

Solicitation Approaches. Ninety-five percent of the agencies initiated the arrangement to use the facilities of religious congregations. Fifty-six percent noted that a member of the agency staff brokers the arrangement to use facilities, thirty-eight percent of the responding directors said they made the contact, and twenty-five percent use a board member. This finding shows that unlike seeking money, building use is usually solicited by a staff member because this aspect of solicitation seems to be more a programmatic function than an administrative function.

Personal Contacts. Forty-two percent of the respondents noted that the spiritual leader of the congregation is the chief contact person when seeking the use of religious facilities, twenty-three percent reported that a member of the agency who is a church member is the chief contact, and nineteen percent indicated that a church staff member is the chief contact person for facility use. Personal contacts ranked the most important element in agency approaches to use religious facilities at sixty-three percent. Agency board–congregational contacts and the track record and commitment of the congregation ranked next in importance for agencies in their approaches to seek facility support from congregations at fifty-nine percent and fifty-six percent respectively. It must be noted again that receiving assistance from congregations, be it facilities, volunteers, or money, is a person-to-person matter.

CHAPTER FIVE

Is The Future Now?

"Much of our meeting time since our beginning in June has worked around the theme of searching for common ground. We seemed to have come to the understanding that our ['mission'] does indeed go beyond the individual work of each of us and our congregations. To use Brady's term: We seem to have to come to understand that it is time to move beyond individual morality to a "corporate" understanding of how the Biblical message can be made part of all our undertakings."

> Penny Martin—Church and Community Planning Group, Memo, November 14th, 1991.

❐

SUMMARY

Major Pionts of Chapter 5

This chapter sews together five patches of the quilt that I am designing on the relationship between the religious and social service communities.

1. Congregational social service provision and assistance to community agencies led to more involvement in shaping a community ethic.
2. The development of this ethic is slow but has an evolutionary pattern to it.

3. Since devolution of services will force more congregations to the public square, we will see the shaping of the community ethic more clearly.
4. Evidence of this evolutionary pattern is presented with the idea in mind that such patterns probably have prevailed in other places but we have not had the definitive research to prove that point conclusively.
5. The new welfare reform will create more patterns like those presented here.

❏

FROM CHARITY TO JUSTICE

The broader implications of these new and not so new relationships presented in chapter 4 are not fully understood. But several aspects of the relationship between the religious community and the social service community have become more focused. First, the longstanding partnership between the religious community and the social service community has an evolving and developmental character to it. The connection between these two systems, and the immeasurable interactions and activities among the people over time, give shape and form to the character of any given community social service system. So, on one level, it would be difficult but not impossible to make comparisons between different communities' service systems.

In Chapters 3 and 4, I noted that congregations spawned development of secular nonprofit and even public agencies. In Chapter 4, I also showed that the same phenomenon was discovered in the Cnaan (1997) study. One of the conclusions that we can comfortably draw from these similar activities is that in geographically and culturally different communities, some congregations are in fact places where religious precepts evolve into a community ethic and take form in an organized, and what eventually becomes institutionalized response to a particular concern or set of concerns. In Chapter 1, I noted:

> Since its [Red Cross] inception in this community [Greensboro], three members of the clergy have been members of its board of directors' executive committee. This means that in eighty years of the Red Cross's life in this community it has representation from most of congregations in the community on its executive committee of the board. The congregations and the Red Cross are like cousins.

In my 1992–95 study, the service activity reported by most agencies was community education. Therefore it is safe to conclude *that there is a continually evolving spiritual life of a community that takes form in the interchange of individual and collective actions of caring for others. Congregation and agency alike have institutionalized ways to nourish and nurture that spirit.* This is illustrated in the calendar in figure 5.1 from Common Ground in Atlanta.

FIGURE 5.1

Example of How Civil Society Blends the Secular and Religious: Common Ground of Atlanta Calendar for February 1995

COMMON GROUND - ATLANTA
MEAL CALANDER

FEB '95

Monday	Tuesday	Wednesday	Thursday	Friday
		1 FEDERAL HOME LOAN	2 ST MARK	3 CLOSED
6 UUCA	7 SHEARITH ISRAEL	8 SACRED HEART	9 CENTRAL	10 CLOSED
13 NW PRES	14 MORNINGSIDE PRES	15 UNITY NORTH	16 REDEEMER LUTHERAN	17 CLOSED
20 NW UU	21 FIRST PRES	22 TEMPLE EMANU'EL	23 OAK GROVE	24 CLOSED
27 EBENEZER	28 FIRST MCC			

The first entry to serve meals at this agency is Federal Home Loan, while the rest are from synagogues and churches. The story behind the entry is both simple and profound. The woman who wanted to get her church involved happened to tell her colleagues at work about the project and they said that they would also like to serve a meal once a month on behalf of their employer—Federal Home Loan. She did not set out to recruit them. The calendar is evidence of how the religious and secular mingle at the agency and community level. Some might see this as blurring of religious and secular, and that may be so. On another level, one might want to consider that our secular laws regarding stealing or murder are the blurring of secular and religious and that the expression of religious precepts become secular only in language but not in essence.

These kinds of interchanges have many tiers to them. One tier sustains individual volunteers. Another gives broader purpose to institutions, such as involved congregations, and still another connects social service agencies to the general community. Providing the infrastructure for community education and, in addition, their direct service provisions with volunteers and money, congregations move deep into various levels of community affairs on personal and institutional levels. The Reagan budget cuts hit all community systems. In theory, the budget cutting policy was the will of the majority. Nevertheless, there were the different congregational responses representing a new involvement in the community as a result of that policy. The responses in figure 5.2 were taken from the transcripts of a focus group I conducted during my 1992–1995 study. Tom's congregation started its community involvement in 1980. Joanne's congregation gained a new awareness of its community role. Loretha's congregation started involvement in the 1970s. John's congregation had been involved in the community, but the policy of decentralization changed the awareness of its community responsibility.

While it is clear from the presentation of the data in the last chapter that the Reagan policies had an actual local impact on the philanthropic activities of people in congregations, the more important aspect of the data is the compelling sense of a duty that congregations felt to help others. The Reagan policy shift reawakened, but did not create that spirit. In the process of that reawakening came a new individual, institutional, and community understanding of social problems and a new understanding within congregations of their capacity to remedy those problems. Volunteers carry a congregation's mission and spirit from congregation to agency, from agency back to congregation, and into the core of the community ethos. It takes more than volunteers to make an institutional interconnection, but **they are essential in building a broader sense of community.**

With the new wave of budget cuts and devolving of services back to the states and localities, the national press is now trying its best to get a handle on what role the religious community is playing and will play in the new welfare reform.

A December 12, 1998 *Chronicle of Philanthropy* (the newspaper of the nonprofit world) cover article "Faith Based Charities To The Rescue?" along with its photo of Reverend Ronald K. Moore, who runs Mississippi's Faith and Families Program, a state-run program designed to link congregations and welfare families, demonstrates an important point. The headline is

---

FIGURE 5.2.

Excerpts From Case Studies of 1992-1995 Greensboro Research.

Question: How Long Do You Think Your Congregation Has Been Promoting Volunteer Involvement?

Tom: Since 1980.

Joanne: Ronald Reagan. I think that's when we adopted a different philosophy: government can't do it anymore, is not going to do it anymore, and it was an encouragement to people to work in the community.

Loretha: I see in our congregation, basically a handful of people actually getting involved in doing the work, but, there is very strong commitment to providing financial resources when the call goes out. Actually people who have the time or can commit the time, go out and do the work. I think that probably started somewhere during the late seventies, or early eighties.

John: As I see it, and I can't pin down an exact date, but, with the emerging need for volunteerism, which stemmed to some extent, from the Reagan Administration's decentralizing a lot of responsibility, imposing on a lot of institutions, putting a lot of people on the street and so on. With the needs increasing the way they have, I think we have more volunteers at our church today than we've ever had. And we need more. It all stems from recognizing a need and attempting to meet it (and) providing financial resources when the call goes out.

---

telling and the question mark even more so. Because there has been little in the way of research to guide the press, reporters don't know that the religious community alone cannot rescue those in poverty, or at least they are not sure. Reporters essentially follow their ears, and it has been conservative political reasoning that has shaped the public discourse over the years. The story also omitted something important. Nothing was mentioned in detail about the concept of a community system of services that must work together, and that partnerships among the actors trying to solve, manage, and prevent poverty must be sustained and nurtured.

Instead, the analysis boiled down to an examination of religion's role in stimulating individual transformation and that different sects must dispense with the differences they had in the welfare reform debate and pull together to help the poor. The subtext of such a view is that a united faith community working together on behalf of the poor can lead people out of their fall from poverty which was caused by their self-induced fall from grace. For years the analysis regarding the cause of poverty has been focused in part on the largess of the bureaucracy which promoted laziness in the welfare recipient. The way up for these individuals was for them to be helped instead by a united faith community. In searching for the reason why the Faith and Families program in Mississippi is not receiving the referrals it had hoped for, the author of the article, Paul Demko (1997) indirectly quotes Reverend Ronald K. Moore, director of the Mississippi program: "Mr Moore blames the slow start on state caseworkers who have been reluctant, he says, to refer people to Faith and Families for fear of losing their jobs as the welfare rolls dwindle." The press and Reverend Moore may reducing the analysis to plausible but not necessarily correct interpretation.

The data in the previous chapter shows that the faith community, the secular nonprofit, and the public system of social services have a complex relationship that helps people with their problems. Personal transformation is an element in social change but there is more to it. Creating a community ethos of care and sealing it through various institutional expressions of faith is another ingredient. We have enough data now from such studies as the Independent Sector study (Hodgkinson et al. 1993), the Orr et.al. study (1994) the Sherman studies (1995, 1997 a, b), and the Cnaan study (1997) to demonstrate that the complex relationships between congregation and community play a role in the transformation experiences of individuals and that complex relationship has to be nurtured and developed if faith-based service organizations are to be successful in stimulating personal transformation. There is probably more going on in Mississippi than the reluctance of caseworkers to refer people to the program because they are afraid to lose their jobs.

Reconsider the offering of facilities by congregations in my study noted in the last chapter, for example. When congregations offer their facilities and resources to a community social agency, they actually donate a special membership into the broader spiritual community of their congregations. By doing so they acknowledge their own institutional commitment to the broader community. The historical legacy of these sustained institutional gifts should not be overlooked, because in effect they sculpt an institutional ethic of care by continued long-term involvement in community life. Maybe caseworkers and congregations in Mississippi have not done the right things to foster long-term commitments. This commitment to community as illustrated in chapter 4 has another side to it. It gives agencies a sense of entitlement to solicit congregational support. But it appears that congregations just don't randomly offer their resources.

The process is more thoughtful, with levels of agreements on roles and responsibilities. It may contractual, as in the case of the Red Cross, one agency in my study. It may be moral as in the case of agencies that do not use formal contracts like the Shepherd Center, which was part of my study. With other agencies still, such as the Black Child Development Institute, the process begins with the initial membership fee in which congregations become institutional members. Regardless of how agencies and congregations seal their institutional relationships, it is clear that congregations are thoughtfully integrated into an agency's process of development and ongoing operations. And as noted above, there are mechanisms, like volunteer training, contracts, memberships, and interlocking board memberships to ensure that the exchange of information, resources, and values flow smoothly from congregation to agency and community. One might be quick to blame caseworkers, but perhaps the relationships are at an early stage of development in Mississippi and that other stages have to evolve before long-term commitments are made. The Red Cross in Greensboro reserves ministerial positions on its executive committee of its board of directors to ensure a religious presence in the organizational decisionmaking process.

This intertwining is not a stagnant process. It is evolving, and as such these institutional relationships have different forms in different times, as seen with the substantial increase of new agencies created from congregational efforts in the Reagan years, the increased volunteer efforts during that time, and the substantial increase in giving money to agencies in the 1980s and 1990s. Policy changes will always affect local efforts.

This ebb and flow of relationships might be better viewed from the context of the stages of policy development that the country has moved through in the last thirty years. Before the Reagan cuts of the 1980s, congregational social services were a backdrop to large-scale federal programs that expanded in the Johnson and Nixon years. They were essential, but they did not play the role they have played during the last two decades or are being asked to play now in welfare reform. Because Reagan's policy of new federalism unfolded more slowly than anticipated, and because congregations quietly became more enmeshed in local service development, they were not seen as the central factor that would make or break a large-scale policy effort as they are seen now.

SOME QUESTIONS

Two questions need to be asked about the social-service growth of congregations throughout the 1980s: What would the system of services have looked like without those congregations providing all the unheralded support for their communities? And, has their involvement in service provision developed in increments slowly creating an ethic of community service? The answer to the first is speculative. I believe that cities and towns would have been overwhelmed by the poor had it not been for the increased involvement of congregations in the 1980s providing womb-to-tomb help to the needy, both on their own and in partnership with the local system of services in their communities. The second question is a bit more complicated and is the focus of the remainder of this chapter. My thesis is that congregations became more involved in service provision locally throughout the 1980s, and have become more inclined to participate institutionally in community affairs. I liken their involvement in the public square as the local community version of the Good Samaritan. The Community Samaritans not only provide volunteers, money, and space for community programs; they also provide the training grounds for small- and large-scale citizen participation. The Community Samaritans bring a different kind of legitimacy to community social service, one that differs in legitimacy from nonsectarian Samaritan efforts. Their moral grounding, motivation to help the poor, and the actual goods and services they offer make them a new force in the public sphere where these partnerships unfold. Over the years, they seem to have moved from mere service provision to participation in the local policy process with a sense of entitlement toward shaping those affairs.

The transition of mainline religious communities into a solid place in the public sphere did not happen overnight. Instead it evolved slowly from de facto, decentralized offerings of individual congregations, to increased collaborative efforts, and to various forms of community partnerships. While the actual nuts and bolts of these partnerships will be discussed more fully later on, the important point here is that evidence of the policy-shaping role of the religious community is right in front of us. The data from the last chapter might be used again as evidence that congregations give resources to the system of services, and the description of some preliminary findings from some earlier exploratory analysis I undertook, points to the possibility that in exchange for their good and services, they use their moral authority to continue to shape the values of community policy. When viewed outside of the quiet but enduring involvement of congregations in community affairs, their current policy-shaping role might be seen as ad hoc and disjointed. Yet, when this process is viewed as a journey of evolving participation, then policy-shaping is a natural outcome of providing more services. The simple rule of local social service policy development is that those who provide the gold, shape and mold the rules. Even though to most observers the process will proceed largely unnoticed and uncharted, it is actually very clear.

More than anyone might have predicted, congregations are and have been making substantial contributions to agencies. Their contributions have evolved over the years from providing volunteers and use of their facilities, to a more comprehensive relationship. They have become much more visible in broader community affairs, especially as they relate to social services. It is quite possible that adding money and other contributions to agency operations compelled them to become not only larger stakeholders in agency operations, but stakeholders in broader community affairs as well. There is some coincidental evidence to support this idea. Agencies report that the largest service function within the range of human service activities agencies is community education—just over 50 percent. Agencies are using buildings, volunteers, and money from congregations to support this activity and other services as well. This moves congregations deep into various levels of community affairs on the personal and institutional levels. Their sense of entitlement toward shaping those affairs is illustrated in the picture shown below (see figure 5.3) of the 1991 march on county government. Sometimes there is a price to pay politically in cutting government programs that work well, make sense, and help people. The April 21, 1991 march for health care, for democracy, and for fairness in government was the result of an organizing effort of the White and Black mainline religious community to protest health care cuts to indigent children proposed by county commissioners. A week before the march, an editorial appeared in the *Greensboro News and Record* (Figure 5.4) from Reverend Otis Harriston of Shiloh Baptist Church arguing publicly with a county commissioner about the role churches have played in helping the poor and questioning the fairness of the cuts to poor children.

Increasingly, as local congregations become educated about what can and cannot be accomplished through their private efforts, the likelihood of such interchanges and protests will increase.

Reverend Harriston's 1991 editorial is only part of the story. Another part is that the religious community, in an unceremonious and Samaritan-like way, was involved with the Health Department in concrete service provision, as well as numerous other services in the community. The protest march was not over some abstract thing called "budget cuts" but was about cuts to children who were being served by the partnership between the government and the religious community. In an April 15, 1991 survey measuring voters preferences in Guilford County (Greensboro is the county seat), close to 60 percent of the voters surveyed were in fact willing to increase taxes for indigent health care services (Bernick and Pratto, 1991). Reverend Harriston's editorial was his entrance into the public debate. His rhetorical tactics were simple: He said these are the services we have provided, and we are going to talk about the larger injustices taking place, not merely to church members, but to the children in the general community. While congregants marched and pastors wrote letters, more structured work was evolving at the local congregational level within the mainline White and Black religious community.

OVERCOMING THE CONCEPTUAL PROBLEM

Because of the Reagan and Bush policy shift, human services have become more locally focused, and more often than not have survived by piecing together operations with fewer federal resources. Two major changes resulted. One, community service systems and people were hurt by Reagan/Bush budget cuts. Two, those same community systems were buoyed

FIGURE 5.3.

Picture of April 21 Protest March.

The March was organized by the religious community of Greensboro, NC. The picture appeared in the September 21, 1991 edition of *The Greensboro News and Record* regarding a series on children's health.

Reprinted with the permission of the *News and Record.*

and thus altered significantly by assistance from the religious quarter—changing permanently the character of the relationship between congregations and their communities.

Initially, more local people started volunteering to solve community problems and did so under the auspices of their congregations. In addition, the congregations through which they volunteered participated "institutionally" in community efforts to tackle problems through the commitment of congregational resources. Habitat for Humanity is a well-known avenue for the individual and institutional effort to help solve social problems.

Examples of congregational involvement throughout the 1980s and 1990s found in local news stories point to a new and interesting set of relationships among community service agencies, government, and religious congregations. More than four hundred local news accounts of local congregational involvement were examined in my research during the last fifteen years. Newspapers in the six U.S. cities illustrated that throughout the eighties to the present, numerous religious groups have been involved in projects ranging from helping the homeless to working with AIDS patients. Perhaps the shrinking welfare state in both western and central Europe has created new relationships between congregations and service providers in the nonprofit sector there as well. The changes in the United States, at least, have sowed seeds for different relationships among secular, sectarian, and interfaith service agencies, and religious congregations.

There are important questions about what these changes mean. For example, will congregational involvement be permanent in both good and bad economic times? Will their roles in service provision decline with the change in parties at national, state, and local level? Are models of cooperation between local governments and congregations varied across communities? Is there really an emergence of a community ethic regarding service as I claim? Are mainline congregations becoming moral and/or political forces locally? But even before exploring those questions, it is important to put the increased activities of congregations in local human services into a theoretical, historically connected, policy-focused, and to some degree empirical framework. Then the emerging pieces of the local congregational and service quilt can better stitched together.

SOCIAL THEORY: CONGREGATIONS AS OPEN SYSTEMS

While there are a number of theoretical frameworks that can be used to view the reemergence of religious congregations as service providers, an open systems perspective offers the greatest insight. A close examination of the evolution of human services in communities across the United States from the systems perspective yields a changing but continuous thread of religious activity in helping people in need.

FIGURE 5.4

April 13, 1991 Letter to the Editor

The letter, to the Greensboro, NC, *News and Record*, preceded the April 21, 1991 congregational march on county government to restore health services to children.

Compassion for poor

To the editor:

It was a real insult to ministers of the Pulpit Forum for County Commissioner Jackie Manzi to accuse us of being mobilized by County Commissioner Katie Dorsett to protest actions to reduce health care and other services that affect the poor in the county.

The former chairman questioned the integrity of ministers who have been in the forefront in protesting the neglect of the poor and underprivileged. We have not only protested, but we have mobilized our churches to provide and supplement services that are not provided or are inadequately provided by agencies.

Before the Urban Ministry established a "night shelter" for the "street people", St. James Baptist Church provided a place in its church building for these homeless people. Shiloh Baptist Church, St. James Baptist Church and Trinity A.M.E. Zion Church initiated housing projects for low-income families 20 years ago.

Many churches provide food pantries, mini health clinics and numerous assistance programs for the poor regardless of race. We feel the pain of those who suffer indignities and neglect because of being underprivileged.

It is a kind of "false economy" that causes leaders to cut programs for the poor. We ultimately pay far more in incarceration, in hospital costs and in our court system. It also reflects unfavorably on our moral value system when we spend billions exploring space but fail to provide a decent living for those on this "earthly space".

We strongly challenge our Board of County Commissioners to be good stewards of God, and to have concern and compassion for the poor and oppressed of our county.

Otis L. Hairston
Greensboro

The writer is pastor of Shiloh Baptist Church in Greensboro.

Reprinted with the permission of the *News and Record*.

Roozen, McKinney, and Carroll (1984:29), theorists of the public mission orientation of religious congregations, assume that the congregation is an open system. As such, they view local congregations as community institutions having complex and changing relationships with their environment, which provides both limits and possibilities for the congregation. Accordingly, a congregation's style of operation is profoundly influenced by its social context, especially the local community context. Even so, congregations according to Roozen et al. (1984) also have the capacity in a limited way, to march to their own drummers as figure 5.4 shows and thus can influence their environment too.

Moberg (1962) notes that as community social welfare institutions, congregations are agents of social control, social reform, and symbols of continuity providing links between past and present. As community welfare institutions which shape and are shaped by their environments, there should be little wonder that they have filled the gaps left by federal retrenchment in the Reagan years and will continue to do so in communities all across the country. Their proclaimed values of caring for others make them good candidates to provide assistance in the struggle against hunger, homelessness, AIDS, and other concerns witnessed right at their doorsteps. If the secular public agencies and private nonprofit agencies with programs that were hit by the budget cuts of the 1980s are also seen as part of a larger but connected system of local welfare institutions aimed at helping those in need, then as cuts inhibited the larger system's capacity to help, congregations expanded to fulfill their own social welfare function and the broader community's welfare needs, too. Roozen et al.'s views help outline the social parameters of the changes, but still leave us a range of questions about changes in policy and program development as a result of stepped-up congregational involvement in service provision. Later in this chapter, I will come back to Roozen et al.'s (1984) typology on congregational mission to help explain the service evolution of the congregations in the Church and Community Forum.

TOWARD AN UNDERSTANDING OF LOCAL INVOLVEMENT

Is there any evidence that congregational involvement locally evolves in discernible stages, or is the involvement just haphazard? During the late 1980s and early 1990s, after conducting two case studies examining congregational involvement for an outreach project of Greensboro Urban Ministry (Wineburg and Wineburg 1986, 1987), an interfaith multiservice organization supported by more than two hundred Greensboro congregations, I surveyed those congregations to determine their level of support for community agencies including Greensboro Urban Ministry, which was a co-sponsor of the project. A synopsis of those findings is in chapter 3. Because I worked in conjunction with Greensboro Urban Ministry, and continually updated staff members of the preliminary results, I was asked regularly to give presentations to church groups and consult with other denominational service organizations, like the Greensboro Episcopal Housing Ministry, the Franciscan Center, American Friends Service Committee, and The Salvation Army.

Soon after the march shown in figure 5.3, six congregations held a forum in order to inform their parishioners of the local county government's cuts in health services to indigent children. I was asked to be a panelist for that forum, and afterward, I was asked to join the group's steering committee where I stayed a member from 1991–1994. While the purpose of the group was continuously evolving, the main intent was to educate their own congregants of major community health and social service matters. The group comprised the six pastors and two parishioners from each of the largest Baptist, Presbyterian, Lutheran, Episcopal, Methodist, and Catholic congregations in Greensboro; myself; the Director of Greensboro Urban Ministry; and a professor from a local college known in Greensboro for his mediation skills. Initially called Greensboro Church and Community Ambassadors (see figure 5.5), the group changed its name to Church and Community Forum. Individually, each congregation fit neatly into Roozen et al.'s (1984) typology of the congregation with the civic mission orientation:

> ... civic congregations are more comfortable with, even affirming of dominate social, political and economic structures; less willing to accept, even opposed to, the use of confrontational techniques in the service of change.... If members choose to involve themselves in public issues, it is as individuals that they do so and not as representatives of the congregation. The same applies to the minister, priest, or rabbi. (Roozen et al. (1984), 35)

During my three years of involvement with this group, I had been a participant in their planning sessions. Many early sessions were mired in the

---

FIGURE 5.5

Mission Statement

The Greensboro Church & Community Ambassadors have come together to seek God's direction for ourselves, our churches, and this organization to:

1) Build bridges into our community to improve human conditions through examining and addressing the causes, not effects, of given problems.
2) Educate ourselves to raise our consciousness so that we can address these issues with our families, friends, co-workers, faith communities, public and private sector organizations, elected representatives and other community leaders-wherever the Judeo/Christian teachings lead us.
3) Align ourselves by finding the common ground that provides new arenas for our ministries.
4) Actively carry out this work through such methods as ecumenical worship opportunities, joint church discussion groups, public meetings, interaction with administrative and/or elected officials, and coordination with other community groups and organizations where our efforts can be effective.

* As of January, 1992, composed of ministers and lay members of the congregations of First Baptist, First Lutheran, First Presbyterian, Holy Trinity Episcopal, St. Pius X Catholic and West Market United Methodist Church of Greensboro NC; and other concerned community representatives.

---

struggle for self-definition (see figure 5.5). These six churches wanted desperately to have a moral influence beyond the walls of their own parishes, and struggled to move from defining their own individual relationship to the local community to a collective definition. While all the congregations were "Civic Oriented" according to Roozen's typology, meaning that they were not going to stir up trouble, the combination of their working together on community issues, their desire to work with Black congregations that had been struggling more openly in the political arena against the local budget cuts for health services to children, and their growing understanding of the complexities of the social and political issues facing the local community moved this group to hold four educational forums in just over a year for the general Greensboro community and the church membership of the six sponsoring congregations. For the fourth forum they reached out and held the forum in co-sponsorship with the Quality of Life and Budget Coalition. This group was made up of members the Pulpit Forum, the umbrella organization of Black congregations in Greensboro, and several more activist White religious congregations and sectarian groups.

The topic of the forum—"Faith Family Values & The Election"—is meaningful because the congregations varied in their responses to the national debate on family values that was going on at that time. Greensboro is a conservative southern city which attracted both the Democratic and Republican presidential candidates in the 1992 election year. Nevertheless, in the context of the local debate on family values at the time, this coalition of congregations had clearly sided with the more activist Black and White ministers of the Coalition for the Quality of life. Collectively, the members of the Church and Community Forum moved in a direction that may have been much more difficult for some or all to do individually.

A THEORETICAL ATTEMPT TO UNDERSTAND THIS INVOLVEMENT

As noted above, news accounts of political involvement of congregations in human service matters showed that congregational leaders were increasingly becoming involved in broader community issues (See also Mitchell, 1990; French, 1991; and Weintraub,1992). But those accounts only casually alluded to what might have been an underlying reason for increased political involvement. I would like to offer the following thesis as the reason for increased congregational involvement in the political aspects of service development. Parts of it have been stated throughout this book.

During the 1980s the religious right captured the air-waves and the national discussion about morality. It was, however, the more mainline congregations who were unceremoniously delivering services as the federal government reduced social spending. States and localities, themselves hit by two recessions in the 1980s and early 1990s, had fewer resources to allocate for social services. Consequently, congregations, mainly the ones with the "civic" mission orientation (as noted above), provided money, people, facilities, and goods to assist in services.

The growth in social problems like AIDS, homelessness, youth crime, and substance abuse, combined with shrinking public resources forced two things: (1) institutional commitment by congregations to become involved in unwritten community partnerships to solve and manage these problems; and (2) individual volunteers and leaders from congregations learning first-hand of the complexities of problems of welfare, homelessness, and the like. As a result, individual congregants became much better versed in the social problems and service issues of the day. And, congregations had increasing community interests because they had been working together with other congregations and service providers in a community partnership. Together, congregants and congregations began developing a broader understanding of community problems. Consequently, through sober reflection on their capacity to respond to demands, and a sense of entitlement to speak about the course of service matters due to their increased understanding and sustained community involvement, they had slowly and collectively moved toward what Roozen et al. (1984) call the activist mission orientation. In other words, congregations not only had been influenced by their social context, but in fact had been shaping it as well (Roozen et al. 1984).

For the activist church or synagogue, achievement of a more just and humane society is a high priority, and the posture toward the existing social and economic order tends to be rather critical. Lines between public or community life and private or congregational concerns are somewhat blurred as community issues are brought into the internal life and program of the congregation as matters of great importance. The congregation is understood as a corporate participant in community life and the rabbi or pastor is expected to be a public figure free to express his or her views within the congregation and the community at large. Social action efforts are endorsed and supported by members with time and funds (Roozen et al. 1984).

Let it be clear that the congregations of the Church and Community Forum had moved slowly and cautiously, but in an activist direction. Early in the group's development, members invited three Black ministerial leaders, each of whom led a considerably more activist congregation than any of theirs, to attend the several planning sessions before deciding to join in the larger coalition. In fact, one minister was the Associate Pastor of Shiloh Baptist Church, the church where Reverend Harriston was senior pastor.

The way in which the Black pastors invoked scripture to stimulate movement by Church and Community Forum members toward an activist orientation is fascinating and clearly a topic for another discussion. In general,
as open systems there was flexibility for the congregational development of
the six churches here to move from a civic to a more activist public mission
orientation because of a number of factors, an important one being the help
of Black pastors.

TOWARD EMPIRICAL VERIFICATION

In 1988–89, as noted in chapter 3, I conducted a survey of congregational
involvement in supporting service activities of Greensboro Urban Ministry
through volunteers and giving money. The questionnaire was designed to
measure involvement in three periods, 1968–1988, 1989–90, and their self-
reported plans for future involvement, 1990 and beyond. This was the question I looked at: *What made these churches different from the other mainline,
civic oriented congregations in the community who had not joined forces by
coming together and offering forums on issues facing the local community?*
The complete answer would have required a new study and taken into consideration the relationship of these congregations to the Black community.
I thought that perhaps there would be some clues in my 1988–89 study as to
why the member churches of the Church and Community Forum moved
to this new level of involvement and a clear collective jump into the activist
realm of mission orientation. To me, those clues meant determining if there
was any hint whatsoever that providing service, in the form of volunteers,
and giving money, was correlated with the level of involvement in community affairs that related to social services policy.

To make the analysis, I made the Forum members one group, while all
the other congregations that responded constituted the other group. The
two groups differed significantly on every measure when comparing their
levels of volunteering and contributing money to Urban Ministry's six programs during the two times measured.

This finding points to the *possibility* that there might be a measurable
factor that moved congregations of the Church and Community Forum
from their civic mission orientation to a more activist orientation, which is

their long-term community involvement in service provision through volunteering and giving money. Much more research needs to be conducted before any definitive conclusions can be drawn about the mediating role a community agency plays in stimulating the development of community involvement, especially when the numbers are so small. However, placing these findings about the Church and Community Forum against the backdrop of congregations nationwide, increasing both their service involvement and political activities, the thesis presented above is quite plausible. In Greensboro, at least, it appears that a combination of factors contributed to the discernible evolution of the civic-oriented Church and Community Forum members into a more activist orientation including budget cuts; a mean-spirited county commission making cuts to children in a distasteful way to a number of organizations including the six churches in this study; a group of activist Black ministers working diligently and patiently with the Church and Community Forum members; and a time in the historical development of community services that makes it propitious for the reemergence of congregations as key players in service provision.

Even with all of the above being plausible, it is quite possible that another important factor in creating this shift in activity has been the long-standing service involvement that these congregations have had in the broader community as reflected through their service to Greensboro Urban Ministry and the range of other agencies in Greensboro. Berger and Neuhaus (1977) point to the roles mediating structures play in empowering people. It may be the case that continual service in the programs of Greensboro Urban Ministry was a factor in empowering the Church and Community Forum members, as a corporate body, to move from a civic mission orientation to a more activist mission orientation. One thing seems certain: Roozen et al.'s (1984) typology is fluid. Given the factors noted above, it is clear that congregations can move from one mission orientation to another. This is extremely important knowledge for service planners working with congregations and a topic for more research.

While this is certainly an understudied topic, it is still clear from the work here that congregations are concerned about the local implications of policy changes and matters of service development. Regarding the question raised earlier about the emergence of a community ethic, it appears that the congregations are sowing the seeds to have a moral say in a broader community interchange on welfare matters. Considering their political clout, they are inching toward understanding their role as power brokers in local welfare matters because of both their moral voice and their resources. While the history of congregational involvement in local service provision is continuous, and that involvement has been shaped by national policies and will continue to be influenced by them, for the foreseeable future congregational involvement will grow.

The very preliminary findings noted here serve notice to the scholars who study denominational activities and social policy that there is much to be learned from studying the intersection of domestic social policy, human service program development, and congregational giving. Given the fact that churches and denominationally tied institutions currently have become central to the operation of local service networks, commanding nearly two-thirds of all contributions, 34 percent of all volunteer labor, and 10 percent of all wages and salaries in the nonprofit sector (Dobkin Hall, 1990:38), their involvement in service provision can no longer be ignored. Is future is now? Yes, and it has been so for a while.

CHAPTER SIX

The Future Ain't What It Used To Be, Or Is It?

Welfare policy, is about history, tradition, social service development, power politics, labor economics, rhetoric, retention and distribution of wealth, and corporate handouts—to cite several aspects not explored deeply or deeply enough by those calling for religious involvement. Consequently, the calls for a church-state partnership are void of any theory or analysis of how social service systems really work at the local level where partnerships operate. Who is to blame?

❐

SUMMARY

Major Points of Chapter 6

1. In order to understand the changes facing communities, we need a variety of research tools to grasp the total picture because the picture is complex.
2. Welfare Reform for the community system of services is really about job retention.
3. Local organizations must form partnerships to succeed in handling their new responsibilities to provide job retention services

❑

The purpose of this chapter is threefold. First, it is intended to build on the discussion in the last chapter about the role the religious community is assuming in the rapidly changing landscape of social services introduced by the policy of devolution. I use devolution in this chapter to mean handing back the design, delivery, and financing of social services to states and localities, something I have tried to show has been happening since the Reagan years. The emphasis will focus on how the devolution of services is creating new, interesting, and sometimes awkward relationships among politicians, social service providers in the public service arena, and the religious community. The tone of the chapter will reflect both my skepticism of the common assumption held by many politicians on both sides of the aisle that religious charities and congregations have the capacity and desire to pick up the slack in service provision and my doubts that the academic community or the press really understand the magnitude of the changes unfolding.

Scholarly disciplines are, in one sense, like medieval fiefdoms. In another era, the isolation and protection that separated the disciplines may have been useful. In this era of rapid change and fast-paced activity taking place at the intersection of politics, religion, and social services there is a need for a broad interdisciplinary discussion, based on active listening and dialogue instead of academic and disciplinary insularity.

Second, this chapter will again give form, through illustrations from the media and other primary documents, to the broad concept: "the changing polity." Here the changing polity will mean that all our realms of social and public life are in the midst of great change. For scholarship to be relevant, it must find new ways to explore this change and inform society about its impact. Even our methods for understanding and interpreting this new reality must be transformed.

In this part of the chapter, I will include primary documents and excerpts from firsthand conversations as they relate to the impact of reform nationally, and especially in North Carolina. This is certainly not the conventional way to handle scholarship, but the vast and rapid changes happening everywhere are both similar and different at the same time, and are forcing scholars to take what I call the ping pong approach to policy analysis, theory building, and understanding change. We currently do not have an official protocol to follow.

On one side of the theoretical net we have a new social policy that affects every locality in the country. Scholars can easily deduce that welfare reform policy has had a major impact nationally by monitoring and assessing the activities of entities whose tentacles touch institutions at the regional, state, and local levels. Such entities include the federal government, especially HUD, national associations like the American Public Welfare Association, The National Association of Counties, United Ways, foundations like the Lilly Endowment and the Kellogg Foundation, liberal and conservative think tanks, and national sectarian charities. In turn, these groups have sharpened their focus on how the policy changes are affecting state and local institutions. My research methods have centered on some aspects of this big picture in that I have monitored the activities of Catholic Charities USA, Salvation Army USA, United Way America, and The Urban Institute through personal and telephone interviews with national staff and collected organizational documents pertaining to the policy shifts. I am a frequent visitor to the web sites of national associations, and follow media activities about welfare reform in Washington and around the country. Such an approach allows for an informed but general analysis, which can hit the big target and still be off the mark regarding the local scene. My local research helps balance this out but may not yield the same results as research on other localities.

On the other side of the net in the ping pong approach to theory building is gauging the affects of the policy shifts on local systems of services. This is a complicated feat because the range of institutions, organizations, and people that the policy hits in these systems is clearly overwhelming. It is just at this point where we need general outlines to guide us, and yet it is precisely here that the deductive process has to give way to an inductive approach to research. We need the case examples to inform theory because the general map no longer serves as a guidepost for understanding the local territory. The question becomes how can scholars get enough data from case examples in a rapidly decentralizing system to validate generalizations of how this major policy change is taking form in different localities?

It is only when there are enough case examples with similar attributes that cross through similar venues, in different localities around the country, that we can say for certain that the policy has made an impact. When such a study has been accomplished, we can glean an insight into the changing polity. Unless we work toward a common language, common sets of research protocols and a general respect for different academic perspectives on the same phenomena, our scholarship will be reduced to solipsism and our understanding of social reality will be so exceptional that it will be irrelevant.

The work in this second part of this chapter also draws on participant observation, key informant research, analysis of primary documents, and program evaluation as it pertains to different dimensions of welfare reform as that reform impacts clients, social workers, public and private agencies, foundations, associations, and religious congregations. I was part of the Governor of North Carolina's Task Force on Community Initiatives regarding welfare reform, or Work First, as it is called in North Carolina. I have been a consultant to and participant with the Mecklenburg County Department of Social services which I will note more about shortly. I have worked very closely with the North Carolina Council of Churches in its monitoring and survey efforts to examine the different ways the welfare reform efforts in North Carolina have affected local congregations and their communities across the state. This effort has enabled me to work with and analyze the efforts of major North Carolina foundations in responding to the changing landscape. I have collected news stories from around the nation, the state of North Carolina, and especially my local community as illustrated throughout. I have been working with a pastor from the largest local Black religious congregation in helping plan a congregational response to increased demands for services. I interviewed a former student who is a Work First case worker on the front lines of welfare reform in the Guilford County Department of Social Services in Greensboro, North Carolina. She has provided me with primary documents from the state of North Carolina and her department in the broader department of social services. These documents outline the procedures of implementing the new policy and portions of the materials she gave me are included as an illustration later in this chapter.

The third purpose of this chapter will provide some practical suggestions to scholars and practitioners: how to first conceptualize the changes, especially about the role of religious congregations in the public policy sphere; how to talk about the local scene in a common language; and how to enhance their relationships with religious institutions. Without scholars joining in the local partnerships, either through consultation, review, evaluation, or research, we stand little hope at understanding the true meaning of one of the most profound changes in social policy in more than sixty years.

DEVOLUTION, THE CHANGING POLITY, AND THE BIG PICTURE

The cover of the September 9, 1996 *US News & World Report* pictures a beautiful white church set against a gorgeous blue sky backdrop, in what appears to be a pastoral country setting. The photo portrays a sacredness and a slice of Americana that only a Norman Rockwell painting could duplicate. The title "The Faith Factor: Can churches cure America's social ills?"suggests not just an end to welfare as we know it, but a return to welfare as we think we knew it, with the religious community playing the central role in human services—something it never really did to the degree that conservative politicians in this country would like us to believe. There is little doubt that as women face their time limits to receive welfare, as the new welfare reform stipulates and the public agencies can no longer help financially, religious institutions will be called on to provide money and other help for the poor. These families may become our newest class of street people.

In an interview I had with Major Tom Jones of Salvation Army USA in June 1997, he told me that one of the Army's greatest expenses is converting single-occupancy shelters to family shelters. Some states and communities had not waited for the August 1 time limits to take hold and prepared for the changes early on. The *US News* story noted above is about the 1994 Faith and Families initiative designed to link each of Mississippi's 5,500 churches with families on the state's welfare rolls. Three other public and religious partnerships that have been reported in the scholarly literature, Maryland's Community Directed Assisted Program, Hampton Virginia's Family Mentoring Program, and Fairfax County Virginia's new Family Support Program, have been set up to help people make a smooth transition from welfare to work and have gained national attention (Sherman, 1997a, b).

In San Diego, three thousand miles from the programs in the East, Ruby Shamsky (1997), a social worker at the Department of Social Services and Chairperson of the DSS-Congregational Mobilization Team, and the Reverend Booker T. Crenshaw, Co-Chairperson of the DSS-Congregational Mobilization Team, sent a January 14, 1997 letter to pastors (see figure 6.2) and church members which welcomed congregations to join a partnership whose goal is to "create a service delivery system . . . which meet(s) the needs of the community in a manner which promotes self-sufficiency and the development of healthy families and individuals." The San Diego community has developed a nonprofit corporation called All Congregations Together (ACT) where volunteers operate a referral desk at the Department of Social Services to refer people in crisis to places in the community for help with such things as emergency food, shelter, transportation, and basic necessities.

To authorities on the left, faith-based social service has no place in the public sphere. To the experts on the right, faith-based social service is the only elixir for a broken welfare state. For those who are working in the real world, trying to solve the everyday problems of those in need, constructing partnerships with the religious community seems to be an essential way to get help and maintain stability in a time of great programmatic changes.

As noted in the last chapter, there is clear enough evidence from all quarters that a basic infrastructure of religious services exists in every locality nationwide (Cnaan 1997). It is also evident that around the country public agencies are tapping into the religious community for assistance in providing support where they experience deficits (Orr, Miller, Roof and Melton, 1994, p. 16)

DIFFERENT ASSUMPTIONS

Two very different assumptions are at work at the national level that also play out at the local level. On the political and religious right is a set of ideas that works its way rightward on the service grid. It moves rightward from the notion that the religious community should be the main providers of services in communities, to the extreme idea that the religious community should be the only service providers in communities. In the middle of that same grid is the notion that religious charities and congregations are partners in local systems and the changes in policy have forced them to put more on already full plates. At the extreme left, the idea of partnership is

FIGURE 6.1

San Diego Letter, January 14, 1997

County of San Diego

CECIL H. STEFFE
DIRECTOR

IVORY L. JOHNSON
DEPUTY DIRECTOR

DEPARTMENT OF SOCIAL SERVICES
CHILDRENS SERVICES BUREAU
1255 IMPERIAL AVENUE, SAN DIEGO, CALIFORNIA 92101-7439

January 14, 1997

Dear Pastor / Church Member:

In July 1996, the San Diego County, Department of Social Services (DSS) implemented the Family Resource Center specifically designed to serve families in the 92101, 92102, and 92113 zip codes. The goal is to create a service delivery system for these areas which meet the needs of the community in a manner which promotes self-sufficiency and the development of healthy individuals and families. The center represents a collaboration between DSS and the community and offers a unique opportunity to blend Government and Community Resources.

As part of this effort, the DSS-Congregational Mobilization Team was formed. The focus of this team is to effectively join resources of Dss, churches, and the community to better help families be self sufficient.

Present team projects include a training (Spring 1997) that will focus on preparing local churches for the impact of welfare reform. We are also in the process of developing a resource directory of churches for the residents of the Family Resource Center area.

We are excited by the community response to our efforts so far. We welcome the participation of church officials and members of congregation of any denomination in the Metropolitan and Southeast San Diego areas.

Please contact one of the chairpersons for more information about the team or to attend our next meeting. We welcome your input and participation!

Sincerely,

RUBY SHAMSKY
Social Worker, Dept. of Social Services
Chairperson, DSS-Congregational Mobilization Team
(619) 338-2597

REV. BOOKER T. CRENSHAW
Co-Chairperson,
DSS-Congregational Mobilization Team
(619) 235-0771

eliminated on the belief that religious entities should not be part of any public social service policy. When these notions play out in the policy arena, money and time get wasted, the discussion of policy centers on character flaws of poor people, or the separation of church and state. As a consequence people needing help suffer. In the practical middle is the Salvation Army who is clearly Evangelical Christian in theology but practical and experienced in local service provision. For them partnerships, are the way to best meet local needs.

Ultimately for ideologues, the accomplishment of political and ideological agendas become far more important than solving urgent social problems. Because this is the loudest discussion going on, the theoretical and ideological realm is an easy place for scholars to hang their hats. It is easier to analyze the ideologies guiding policy than to analyze the gradations of the theories as they bump up against reality. Consequently, few are examining reality and an entire domain of scholarship, and an extremely important one at that, has been left untouched. The unexamined realities of welfare reform get played out daily in the lives of recipients, social workers, clergy, volunteers, public service workers, religious volunteers, employers, mid-and upper-level bureaucrats in local and state governments, community social service systems, large and small sectarian charities and in the media. But these are certainly not all the domains affected by these changes. Below is attempt to capture a slice of the changes as they are hitting North Carolina.

DEVOLUTION NORTH CAROLINA STYLE: THE LITTLER PICTURE

Just five weeks after the *US News* story, an important Associated Press news story appeared in the October 22, 1996 *Greensboro News and Record* entitled: "DSS head: Churches can help reform welfare." Appearing under the caption "Welfare reform goes to church" is a photo of Reverend Ralph Williamson, an associate pastor of Steel Creek AME Zion Church in Charlotte, which is North Carolina's largest city. In addition to being an associate pastor, Reverend Williamson is an employee of the Mecklenburg County Department of Social Services (Charlotte is the county seat), having been transferred from its Division of Children's Services to head an effort aimed at increasing the involvement of the religious community with regard to helping people move from welfare to work

Officials in Charlotte, like those in San Diego and many other places, also recognized, that the transition from the old welfare system to the new one would leave some people in rough circumstances. At the local level, people face the consequences of the policy decisions that get made elsewhere—ones that are often presented in the press as neat, clean theoretical plans that will succeed if given the chance. The new changes in welfare have compelled the Mecklenburg County Department of Social Services to start building an innovative and lasting partnership among North Carolina's welfare reform participants (called Work First), members of the business and educational community, United Way, The City of Charlotte Neighborhood Development Department, and the faith community. They called for a much needed spirit of cooperation, to accomplish this new approach to job preparation, job retention, and the reduction of poverty. As of this writing, there are 14 other communities in North Carolina that now have faith community coordinators.

WELFARE REFORM IS JOB PLACEMENT

Welfare reform's major focus in the public policy sphere is squarely on job placement and minimally on job preparation, something that has been left out of the debate on why welfare needed to be reformed. A job placement policy does not focus on developing careers for poor moms, and trying to get them increasingly higher wages. This policy is about reinforcement of the work ethic in low-income communities and keeping wages low in the low-paying service industry. As such, the conservative business and government alliance shifts tax revenue from welfare programs to incentives and other programs for businesses to hire welfare recipients. An example of this is in North Carolina's Welfare reform shown in Figure 6.4, where local governments chosen to design their own welfare reform can shift 10 percent funds received from the state and put it into infrastructure projects that supposedly will make it more attractive to industry to locate or do business in those counties.

Top North Carolina government officials are seldom concerned about the barriers to keeping a job; they are more often concerned with placing people in jobs. If participants fail to stay employed, it is their own fault. That might be the case in many instances, but the idea of overcoming structural barriers like the lack of job training, transportation, no child care, poor housing, and school problems is now a private responsibility. Such a policy approach strengthens the current conservative analysis that the cause of poverty is personal irresponsibility, reinforced by a bumbling welfare bureaucracy. So if government gets tough, forces people off the dole and into the workplace, and they don't succeed there, then let them work out their problems with the help of local institutions. The religious community as is demonstrated in bullets one, two, and three, of Figure 6.2 (a state document) is being advertised as key in job placement and retention.

Nevertheless, service providers in departments of social services throughout much of the state of North Carolina are keenly aware that there are numerous barriers that keep people with low incomes from *retaining* their jobs and attaining self-sufficiency. Caseworkers, however, are in no position to press for institute changes. Passing the baton from the federal to the state level, with the state now making most of the eligibility rules, has been uneven and confusing.

IN THE TRENCHES

Figure 6.3 is the correspondence I received on February 26, 1997 from a field research associate, Barbara Earls, who heads up the Jubilee project of the North Carolina Council of Churches and represented the Council at the meeting. The information in the box is the synopsis of the remainder of the February 26, 1997 meeting of the Governor's Task Force on Community Initiatives on Welfare Reform. It is included here because the subtext of what was said is very important to understanding the real dynamics of policy-making. The Joe in the box is a Z. Smith Reynolds foundation officer, and chair of the Governor's Task Force on Community Initiatives. His foundation has been instrumental in shaping statewide policy issues. Peter and Kevin are the chief policymakers in North Carolina's Work First instituted by Democratic Governor Jim Hunt.

FIGURE 6.2

Carolina Work First Document

This, the last page of the document, outlines the job retention strategy with the religious community (January 1997).

Helping people become self-sufficient

Religious and community groups across North Carolina are answering the call to help families leave welfare behind for self-support and personal responsibility.

■ In New Hanover County, Work First participants find appropriate clothing for job interviews and practice job interviewing skills through services provided by the Saint Mary's Office of Social Ministry in Wilmington. Employers also meet regularly at Saint Mary's to develop strategies to help Work First participants get jobs.

■ First Baptist Church in Charlotte hosted a job fair, at which a Work First participant found a full-time job in the church's food service department.

■ First Presbyterian Church of Wilson helps Work First participants overcome lack of transportation to work. Members of the church volunteer to transport Work First participants to and from work. Also, the church is one of Wilson County's work site sponsors for Work First participants needing job experience.

■ The American Association of University Women in Henderson County developed a life skills curriculum to share with churches helping Work First participants to acquire job skills.

Still, more organizations are needed to help make Work First work!

For more information or to get involved in Work First, call or write your county's department of social services. Or contact:

Work First
Division of Social Services
NC Department of Human Resources
325 N. Salisbury St.
Raleigh, NC 27603-5905

Statewide Work First hotline, 1-800-724-0583

The North Carolina Department of Human Resources does not discriminate on the basis of race, color, national origin, sex, religion, age or disability in employment or provision of services

100,000 copies of this public document were printed at a cost of $4,051.00 or .04 per copy.

January 1997

The conversation the letter is concerned with concerned the state's job placement policy, which determined who got jobs. Other factors were ignored: job retention, how long they worked, whether they grew in their jobs, how much training was needed, what kinds of other supports were necessary to sustain employment of the most difficult people to keep in jobs, what happened to them if they were eliminated from the program, and how the system of services locally were changing as a result of the policy changes. The state budgeted no money for this policy outcome analysis and wanted the Z. Smith Reynolds Foundation to pick up this portion of the work. The partnership referred to was between the state and the religious community whom the policy officials were assuming would jump right in and provide support without question.

Two other people mentioned, Diana and Vicki, are key to the connection between the religious community and state government, since Diana heads a project of involving rural Black churches and Vicki is the key program officer for North Carolina Work First. While a bureaucrat, she is very astute and sympathetic to the concerns from the religious quarter specifically that they don't want government telling them what to do as had been the case in earlier meetings. Evelyn Mattern is the Director of The North Carolina Council of Churches and the meeting referred to in the box was with the Duke Endowment regarding the development and funding of the Jubilee project of the Council, which is now funded in part by the Endowment, and helps congregations develop capacity to serve, and organizes them to impact policy as well.

A QUICK REVIEW

One point I want to make here is that welfare reform is complicated and the implementation is changing the relationships between institutions and people at every level. Just how those relationships unfold from place-to-place is anyone's guess, but some generalizations are appropriate. Summoning local congregations and religious charities to deliver more of the nation's social services clearly follows the spirit of the Reagan and Bush social policies—captured in George Bush's now famous "Thousand Points

FIGURE 6.3.

**February 1996 Field Report from Barbara Earls,
NC Council of Churches**

Hi, Bob,

Sorry we didn't have much chance to talk about stuff yesterday, and hope your presentation went well last night—long day. What happened after you left was quite amazing. We went on til 4:15, and the 10 or so in the room experienced what happens occasionally when a group of different people enters into one spirit and crosses a line from meeting participants to human beings who connect.

Joe revealed how Peter L. and Kevin F. at a meeting, re: their grant proposal, admitted "the partnership idea isn't working." Eventually the discussion turned to how the whole state plan is bunk, how we in fact have not been doing what's needed to accomplish the appropriate goal (the things we want), and how there needs to be a big statewide commission or whatever on poverty and economic justice.

Were you there when Joe recommended we disband as the subgroup on community involvement? It ended that we would meet one more time—to be clear on next steps that need to be taken by whomever, to address what we really care about. You'll get a message on it. Joe cited the need for research on the effects of the new mess and said you (BW) would be ideal to corral a project on it if you were dean or something (he inferred you were more than capable but too busy already).

He doesn't know about our meeting tomorrow, I guess, and I have not mentioned that to him or Diana or Vicki or anyone. As for tomorrow, Evelyn Mattern, whom you will quickly come to admire, will lead off with the Council's idea on what's needed in general, and set the discussion as an exploration of ideas on how to proceed and fund the thing.

I hope then you can tell your idea, which you started to mention yesterday but which got cut off by the meeting beginning. You are best to conceptualize the project as a whole, I think, and then we can all react with what we see our pieces to be. Does this sound like what you pictured? I feel like I've been hit by a truck and am exhausted these days, but am fairly excited about the prospects here. Sounds like you're busy enough, too. Drive safely tomorrow....

Barbara

of Light" campaign speech that simultaneously called for decreased governmental spending and increased local voluntary support for social welfare efforts. A March 8, 1990 request for new program proposals (*Federal Register* 1990:8555) stated the Reagan/Bush view clearly: "*Human service needs are best defined through institutions and organizations at the local level.*" A major difference between now and then is that now there is a conscious attempt to target religious institutions *specifically* as the local organizations most suited to take the service baton from government. From the available evidence much more careful planning and study needs to go into the process.

We have been witnessing the first two stages in a cycle of reshaping and redeveloping the welfare state: The first stage was the Reagan budget cuts and the Bush push for more nonprofit involvement locally. The second has been more budget cuts, targeting the religious community to step up its involvement in local service development through legislation like Senator Ashcroft's, Charitable Choice provision in the new Welfare Reform (Center For Public Justice 1997) that allows religious congregations to receive federal money. In addition Governors Fordice (Edwards 1995) and (Hunt, *Greensboro News and Record* 1996), have spoken publicly in favor of drawing more service from the religious community in Mississippi and North Carolina.

Two independent forces seem to be converging in this cycle: *Mainline* congregations and religious charities in quiet and inconspicuous ways had been stepping in locally and meeting new demands throughout the 1980s. Even though their role is subsidiary, mainliners succeeded because their roots of service have wound around and through local public and secular service systems from the beginning of nationhood, forming interesting local partnerships and strong community bonds (Monsma 1996). On the other hand, the growing rhetoric, public influence, and political gains of the religious right in the 1990s created an atmosphere in which politicians more and more became increasingly comfortable in making the religious community a focal point in a new social policy.

So when rhetoric turned into implementation, we actually witnessed, as the figure 6.2 above illustrates, *the split between what government and the religious right think and assume the religious community ought to do, and what it is capable and willing to do.* Changes have been guided more by ideology, and frustration with the old policy, than thoughtful study and analysis. Implementation is not as easy as the policymakers had envisioned. The academic community has some responsibility for this quagmire and it members will be increasingly pushed by their communities to respond.

Clearly, North Carolina is a conservative Southern state. But from the looks of who controls the U.S. House of Representatives, the U.S. Senate, governor's seats, and state houses nationally, many other states are conservative as well. What is illustrated below is no anomaly, but an early example of a social policy running its course to its eventual reconfiguration, much the same way the New Deal legislation evolved. The seeds of the changes are in the *implementation* that takes place locally.

LOCAL DEVOLUTION AND THE CHANGING POLITY

In the shift from the federal welfare policy to the state run-welfare reform, the state of North Carolina's legislature designated that 15 percent of the eligible recipients of Work First services (North Carolina's Welfare Reform) could be served in pilot programs where the counties design and deliver services, and determine who is and who is not eligible for help, and for how long (see figure 6.4).

Coordination with the religious community is seen as essential (as I pointed out in figure 6.2), and is part of the government promotional on the program. As of this writing, nine of the twenty-one counties chosen to design their own welfare plan have called on the religious community to be involved in some level of assistance. Statewide, a total of 15 counties have Faith community coordinators. Some of those coordinators are ministers who work for the local department of social services like Reverend Williamson in Charlotte. Others are working with local faith-based ministries. Some are full time and others are part-time

If local systems of service are going to succeed in preventing many people from losing their jobs because of lack of child care, transportation, or housing they need the churches increasingly. In the previous era, there was a public safety net of support if a mom lost a job. National policy has changed that. Now a person can no longer receive any assistance from fed-

FIGURE 6.4

Welfare as We Knew It

Some North Carolina counties can now run their own welfare reform programs

---

Wednesday, October 29, 1997

Counties vie for welfare reform

● Commissioners in at least 22 counties say they want to join North Carolina's welfare experiment.

BY JOHN COCHRAN
Raleigh Bureau

RALEIGH — Nearly a quarter of the state's counties want to be part of an experimental welfare program that would give them unprecedented control over federal and state welfare dollars — and a

"Every county has unique problems," said Larry Potts, chairman of the Davidson County Board of Commissioners. "I'd just like to see a program more closely tailored to Davidson County's needs."

Counties have until Friday to choose one of two options: remain a standard county whose welfare eligibility and criteria standards are set by the state, or gain more authority by becoming a pilot county.

Guilford County commissioners fell one vote short of choosing pilot status earlier this month, so Guilford will operate as a

chance to set the pace of reform statewide.

So far, county commissioners in at least 22 counties — representing a total of about 15,500 welfare families — have voted to apply for a spot in the state's two-year pilot welfare program. In that group are nine Piedmont Triad counties — Forsyth, Randolph, Davidson, Alamance, Davie, Surry, Stokes, Yadkin and Caswell.

The counties chosen for the pilot program will have the authority to decide who qualifies for public assistance and how much help to provide.

standard county.

Counties that decide to apply for pilot status must have a welfare plan to the state by mid-February that details now they would use their new authority. State legislators will choose the pilot counties next spring.

Before then, however, some counties that have voted to apply for the program might find the challenge too daunting and drop out of the running.

Please see **WELFARE,** *Page* **B2**

eral dollars after five years of welfare assistance. In North Carolina there is a five-year limit as well. Once a person has reached a two-year period of assistance, she must be off assistance for minimum of three years before assistance can resume.

Such a shift obviously means that the policy's success rests on the construction of a new partnership between the religious community and local social service agencies responsible for carrying out this policy. The changes caused in the shift of responsibility from the federal and state levels, coupled with fewer dollars, will leave some new holes to be stitched in the safety net for the needy. The nonprofit sector and religious community will have to meet these needs without much new funding. This is an unfunded mandate.

The picture and story about The Reverend Williamson's efforts above and the North Carolina Work First document in figure 6.2 and figure 6.4 below, illustrating the further devolving the design and delivery to the local level, are an early signs of not just the collaborations in large cities, small towns, and even remote rural communities in North Carolina, but a set of examples of the changing polity. In Charlotte, congregational leaders and social services staff have met for two years in a project called *A Faith Community United* to plan for ways to help people most affected by welfare reform.

The gritty details of this organizing effort of the Faith Community United is a subject for a full-length article at least. But it would be wise to note one detail. The same conservative commissioners who voted to end funding for the arts, also decided against being a county that designed welfare service without state guidelines. Simply put, once the commissioners found out how difficult it was making the transition from a federally guided to a state-guided welfare system, and how cautious the religious community was about becoming a full partner, they knew it would be far too chaotic to switch to a county-designed system with so little planning time to make the transition to local operation. They voted to stay under state authority. The devil in devolution is in the details. Interestingly, Mecklenburg County, the county in North Carolina most able to design its own welfare system, opted not to do so. This is an instance where a little bit of practical knowledge of the intricacies of making a full-scale shift in responsibility loses the ideological bite of "more local control." Conservative Republicans who have seen what happens when the intricacies of the policy have to be worked out with local funds and voluntary resources opted to let the state bear the brunt of the responsibility for the success or failure of the policy. Local officials after a solid year of working with local institutions to prepare for the changes, saw how difficult it is to place some people in employment when they have no way to get to the job, how ill-equipped many religious congregations are to handle full-scale welfare responsibilities when the public services can no longer be used, and how unprepared the community college and employment systems are to provide the training to prepare people for twenty-first-century work requirements. Nevertheless many conservatives in medium and smaller counties who have done little or no community planning have not opted for state guidelines. Time will tell who is right.

WHERE DOES THE RELIGIOUS COMMUNITY FIT AND WHAT DOES IT OFFER?

The religious community's importance in the system of local social services will continue to grow because it is a set of community institutions that holds, by far, most of the private charitable resources in an increasingly shrinking pool of such commodities. To be relevant analysts of current policy, scholars in many fields will have to learn about the religious community in relationship to the local social service and political community. In a very important scholarly book, *When Sacred and Secular Mix*, Professor Stephen Monsma (1996) notes on page 3 and 4 that his book is not concerned with all nonprofit organizations, but with those that have primarily public service or public benefit purposes. Monsma uses Lester Salamon's (1992) categorization scheme of the nonprofit sector and thus puts religious *congregations* in a "member benefitting category" noting that they meet essentially for sacramental or worship purposes.

This categorization may be true from a theoretical perspective but at the local level, as I have demonstrated in chapters 4 and 5, congregations have a far more complicated social and political function than mere "member benefitting or sacramental purpose." Below are the seven assets that congregations bring to the local service partnership. Knowing the types of assets and ways to approach the religious community is very important for researchers and social service providers in their quest to conceptualize and redevelop their services in the midst of rapid change. Helping refine and sustain those assets is key for leaders in social services. If localities want successful partnerships that include the faith community, it is crucial to find ways to learn how that community operates. What will be presented here are seven assets that the faith community can contribute to a community partnership.

SEVEN ASSETS

1. Mission To Serve

The first asset the faith community brings to a community partnership is a mission to help the poor. Each major religion is grounded in helping those in need. Before soliciting help from a congregation, volunteer recruiters must recognize that people who come to a particular space for worship consider themselves part of a faith community. When they express their faith through service, they usually help those in need in their immediate congregation first. This does not mean that members of a religious congregation won't reach out into its neighborhood and the wider locality. Congregations do this and have done so increasingly throughout the Reagan and Clinton years (Wineburg, Ahmed, and Sills 1997). But it does mean that when recruiters approach congregations whether it is for research or for resources, those doing the approaching should avoid assuming that congregations are not serving others because it "appears" they are not involved in one or another community project. It might be helpful to find out just what activities congregations are involved in within the congregation and outside as well.

2. Pool of Volunteers

Because faith communities are gathering spots for worship and places where expression of faith takes form, there is a ready-made pool of volunteers. Communication can be done through congregational newsletters, sermons, and adult religious classes. Worthy of note is is that a commitment of volunteers to a project should be recognized as that particular faith community's collective commitment to join in a partnership. The faith community and its individual volunteers need to be nurtured for balance and harmony between often competing interests such as personal needs for satisfaction and congregational capacity to deliver what is asked for. In addition the congregation should have an accurate presentation of what the agency needs from it. These key points can strengthen the institutional and individual bonds. Researchers must consider some of these dimensions if they are to understand the changing polity.

Institutions, especially congregations, have a language they use to define their commitment. Some call it "outreach," others call it "mission" and still others call it "social action." Whatever the term, it usually signifies a faith community's commitment to making a difference (Claman and Butler 1994). There are often committee structures with well-defined processes and procedures that are followed before committing people and other resources to projects, especially if projects are long-term in nature. Practitioners and researchers would do well to learn about the congregations they plan to enlist into service, designing projects and evaluations tailored to the capture the culture and rhythms of those faith communities.

3. Sacred Space

Religious congregations often have extra usable space that agencies could tap into for meetings, community forums, educational, and cultural activities. As often happens, congregations are community spawning ponds for social change—whether it is awareness around health needs of children as has been the case in my community of Greensboro, North Carolina, or organizing marches and protests during the civil rights movement as in many cities in the 1960s. As noted earlier, I found that 18 percent of the existing nonprofit organizations in Greensboro evolved from congregations (Wineburg, et al. 1997). Cnaan's (1997) essential study goes so far as to list the names of nonprofit organizations that emerged from congregations in six cities.

People who use the facilities of the religious community might have a good chance of developing and sustaining long-term relationships with congregations if they stay aware that a faith community expresses more than kindness and generosity when it invites a group or organization to use its facilities. It is an invitation to enter their sacred space, and in a very concrete way it is an offer join in one dimension of their expression of faith. My research shows that an organization's use of religious space increases its chances of securing volunteers from that faith community. Clearly such organizations are more than member-benefitting organizations. They are community-benefitting organizations too (Cnaan 1997).

4. Grant Makers

The fourth asset of the religious community is its potential for raising and distributing discretionary funds for designated causes. In a time when public funds are being cut for service delivery, the religious community has been asked for ever more money to help local service efforts. Fifty-two percent of the agencies in my 1992–1995 (Wineburg 1996b) study of Greensboro had received financial support from local religious congregations and much of that support came during the Reagan years when there were decreases in public funds for social services. Those agencies that receive funds, or for that matter any kind of resource from the religious community, will strengthen their ties by submitting reports and personal stories of how the funds and people helped make a difference. Researchers interested in understanding the full funding picture of local nonprofit agencies must analyze the contributions of the religious community.

5. Political Strength

The religious community holds tremendous potential for political strength if it chooses to use it. In an era of public retrenchment, the religious community holds an important bounty for both the health of local citizens and the careers of politicians. It is important to understand that because of new partnerships happening locally, a new set of relationships are unfolding. The religious community will become more involved in local collaborative service planning with public and nonprofit agency service providers.

Congregations will learn increasingly how, why, and the extent to which social service organizations distribute cash and goods, as well as professional-and volunteer-based services. Researchers should chart these activities in order to get a clear picture of the local nonprofit sector. Members of the religious community will gradually recognize that community problems will not get solved without their participation. Volunteers from congregations, alliances of ministers, employees of religious charities, and their volunteers who also offer goods and services will have increasing leverage over *how* services get delivered and eventually how they are *paid* for as well. As members of religious institutions learn first-hand about the scope of certain problems they will have a deeper understanding of what can be accomplished through private voluntary efforts and what can be done through public efforts.

As Amy Sherman (1995) has emphasized, and this has also been noted above, an important point to understand is that state agencies tend to treat contracting nonprofits not as equals but as subcontracting functionaries doing the government's bidding. However, as congregations participate increasingly in the distribution of services through collaborative arrangements, they will become a political force in shaping the changing roles that public and private nonprofits play in determining community needs. The devolution of services, as shown in the North Carolina instance, will make it difficult if not impossible to chart these changing roles everywhere. Congregations will, however, on one level or another, influence the direction the resulting distribution of goods and services, placement of volunteers, and education of the public will take.

There may be a danger of damaging the prospects of building healthy partnerships if public agencies and some private ones, as well, shove the service baton at the religious community without recognizing that it is a new day in service provision locally, and that the religious community, once seen by some as somewhat tangential to the successful operation of local service systems, is now clearly an essential ingredient for the success of the partnership in solving, managing, and preventing community problems. Scholars and informed practitioners can do much to educate those who do the bargaining. As pivotal institutions in determining the health and vibrancy of community service systems in this new era, religious communities especially at the congregational level must be treated with respect and a true understanding of their growing political strength and importance in the public realm of service and resource provision.

6. Moral Authority

A sixth asset that the religious community brings to the service arena is closely connected to political clout, and that is moral influence. Over the last fifteen years or so, much of the media coverage regarding religion that has made headlines and talk show circuits has been about the Christian Coalition, abortion, prayer in schools, cult-induced mass suicide, scandals like Jim and Tammy Bakker's at Heritage Village, religiously inspired boycotts of Disney products, million men and women marches, and huge Promise Keepers rallies. From that angle it might be easy to conclude that religion in the United States is about capturing the souls of a morally wayward culture. For the most part, while the media have focused on their efforts here people from mainline religious congregations and their charities have been quietly serving soup, building houses, helping refugees, distributing grants, volunteering at hospices and homeless shelters, opening their facilities to the Boy Scouts, Girl Scouts, Red Cross, public school meetings, AA, and to scores of other self-help groups that need meeting space. Their work has become the main patch of a moral quilt that preserves the warmth and vitality of community and neighborhood life in city and town alike around the nation.

All social policy sits on a moral foundation. As social policy development becomes the property of localities, the one commodity the faith community has a monopoly on is moral authority. There is no question in my mind that there will be an early struggle between radicals and moderates over whose morality will shape local policy. Ultimately, it will be those who spend the time in the trenches with the hungry and hurting, those who provide grants and open their facilities to neighborhood and community groups, and those who express their faith through service who will shape the morals of a community. An evangelical church, The Salvation Army's motto for more than 130 years has been "soup, soap and salvation." Those who meet the community's needs with concrete goods and services will shape the moral agenda locally. I pointed to evidence of this in the last chapter. Researchers who want to really understand the mortar of civil society must study the use of facilities of congregations as schools for community education about local problems. They can also help moral leaders of congregations understand the specific causes and possible remedies for problems that their faith communities will tackle.

As congregational representatives attend meetings to wrestle with the complicated problems facing the community, they will become better prepared to make their moral arguments much more strongly. No child should go to bed hungry if there is enough food in a community. No elderly person should have to choose between buying medication and food. No one should freeze to death in a community where there are enough resources for all to be warm. No one should be without shelter when communities have thousands of boarded up houses and apartments. As the religious community continues its service efforts, it will exert increasing moral authority, and start holding those accountable for actions that keep people down rather than lift them up—whether they be elected officials, government bureaucrats, or nonprofit leaders.

7. Creativity and Experimentation

As new partnerships form, there will be a fresh mix of people and institutions trying to solve, manage, and prevent problems. Large bureaucracies, like those that house departments of social services, often have fixed ways of doing things, not necessarily because they are the most effective, but because "that's the way things have been done." Large bureaucracies don't have the same goals as congregations, nor do they have the same souls. Researchers can report about new partnerships and creative ways of doing things, which may in turn encourage experimentation, and cultivate the best blend of the strengths public agencies offer and the desirable assets of the religious community.

The faith community has been touted as a more effective service provider than the public agencies (Olasky 1992) because it can experiment and work on spiritual matters as part of an overall service plan. This may be the case, but if the state relates to the religious community in a rigid and authoritarian way as it does at times with county agencies, the religious community will not be a vital partner in local service provision. The Public Samaritan efforts of the religious community could easily be undermined if it were expected to replace the services lost by cuts to the bureaucracy leaders must to bring that community into the partnership with a realistic new way of operating services.

I can say in good conscience that state government officials in North Carolina are learning how to enlist its voluntary partners from the religious sector in a kinder and gentler way than when they first started out. Yet there will be backslides along the way. As we move further into the era of more locally financed social service systems, it is clear that we will need new ways of solving, managing, and preventing some of the major problems surrounding us. The religious community will not be able to take over the country's social welfare matters on its own. The local system of services will not be able to manage its affairs effectively without assistance from the religious community. A new partnership needs to form. Leaders from the all segments of the community can do much to make sure this partnership flourishes.

In the words of Casey Stengel "The future ain't what it used to be."

CHAPTER SEVEN

A Thought Experiment

Upon one occasion the brothers fell out about something, and Chang knocked Eng down, and then tripped and fell on him, whereupon both clinched and began to beat and gouge each other without mercy. The bystanders interfered, and tried to separate them, but they could not do it, and so allowed them to fight it out. In the end they were both carried to the hospital on one and the same shutter.

> — "The Siamese Twins" by Mark Twain. *A lesson for politicians who continue to view the public system of services as if it were not connected to the private system.*

◻

SUMMARY

The Major Points Points of Chapter 7:

1. The system of services locally is interconnected and intertwined.
2. Any change in one part of the system of services undoubtedly affects the other parts.
3. The thinking that has shaped the development of Reagan policies and now the new welfare reform policies has not taken into account what the policies would do to the interconnected services locally.
4. A thought experiment is presented that likens the system of services to a highway under construction.

5. A framework for understanding the system of services and a framework to understand the role the religious community plays in that system are presented.

❏

In the introduction of this book I quoted a passage from chapter 17 of Charles Murray's *Losing Ground*, in which he called for the following "thought experiment": *"Our final and most ambitious thought experiment consists of scrapping the entire federal welfare and income-support structure."* Much of what I have said to this point shows that the basic assumption underlying Murray's experiment has little to do with the reality that local nonprofit agencies, religious charities, and congregations are all interconnected and that a dramatic change in one connecting link has an important impact on the others. A sad, but real point is that the thinking behind current policy is to make Murray's experiment become reality. What would the effects be?

The data I presented in the previous chapters, and from other studies which I have quoted, such as Cnaan's six-city study, and Orr's Los Angeles study, show that the public and private systems of services in communities are interwoven into a larger system of care. Table 7.1 below is a framework that illustrates rather neat service categories. This presentation is for illustrative purposes only because in reality the system is intertwined, overlapping, and interconnected. The elements in the conceptual framework are dynamic, and responsive to forces of change from within the system and outside as well. At street level, where services get delivered, there is usually far less ideological grandstanding and far more collaboration than one might expect, especially in the case of the religious community working with the pubic and nonsectarian agencies in solving a range of community problems.

The framework shows seven levels of service provision and a snapshot of their funding sources: (1) Public agencies usually receive funds from federal, state, and local taxes; (2) United Way agencies receive funds from individual and corporate giving, solicit grants and contracts from public and private sources, and charge fees; (3) Nonprofit, Non United Way agencies receive funds from individual and corporate giving, solicit grants and contracts from public and private sources as well, and charge fees; (4) Self-Help groups usually receive funds from individual contributions in the form of dues, or simple collections; (5) Religious Congregations receive funds from membership dues, or other local private solicitations; (6) Sectarian Agencies receive funds from individuals, corporations, and religious denominations. They solicit grants and contracts from public and private sources, as well, and charge fees; (7) For Profit Providers receive government contracts and charge fees for services. What follows is the framework and walk-through of each of the categories which also introduces a different kind of thought experiment. After the presentation of the Public and United Way Categories, I will show the religious interconnections, first between the public realm of services and then the United Way services. Here, I want to demonstrate the profound complexity of the relationships between the religious community and two major services entities at the local level, keeping in mind that the entire series of interconnections is even more complex and that policymakers would do their communities a great service to try to enhance the interconnections instead of weaken them. After the explanation of the rest of the participants in the local system of service, a framework for understanding the religious community's role in this larger scheme is presented.

A JOURNEY THROUGH THE PUBLIC REALM

It is now time to show how essential it is to understand the service delivery system locally. The slanted presentation of a bureaucratic welfare system that supports slothful people whose intentions are merely to pick the pockets of law-abiding taxpayers disregards some essential concepts about local service

Table 7.1

Conceptual Framework for Local Service Provision

Type of Service	Funding Sources
Public	Federal, state, local taxes
United Way agencies	United Way, local government funds, grants, contracts, fees
Nonprofit, Non United Way	Grants, contracts, dues, local government funds, fees
Self-help	Dues, local funds
Religious congregations	Local funds
Sectarian and interaith agencies	United Way, local government funds, grants, contracts, fees
For-profit providers	Fees, government contracts

delivery, so let's try a thought experiment of our own. Let's think of the public realm with regard to service delivery as a vast and sometimes incomprehensible system of services that is uniquely American, and rooted in the *good intentions* of both liberal and conservative politicians trying to solve complex and interwoven problems. The recipients of care are often innocent children who, regardless of their parents' behavior, did not cause their own impoverished plight. Let's think of the *system* that serves them, including the elderly, the sick, the disabled, and others, as a superhighway with five lanes on each side of a median, with exits and entrances everywhere. The expressway is crossed by bridges and underpasses, all being fed by major and minor roadways. Like a highway that eventually leads most people to safer and more secure destinations, the system of services in our experiment tries to lead people to safer and more secure destinations in their troubled lives.

This superhighway in our experiment represents our major federal programs weaving their way in and out of the lives of the impoverished, trying to get them to a destination that fosters their independence and self-sufficiency, which, if the programs accomplished their missions, means social stability for the greater society. Programs like Head Start for kids, and the Older American's Act for the elderly, both operating under the auspices of local nonprofit agencies, are but two roadways entering this highway. There are other federal roadways, like The Social Security Administration and Housing and Urban Development Administration, both of which operate federal agencies locally, and constitute other major links in the social welfare highway. One assists in financial security and the other in housing.

Other federal programs, like Food Stamps and Medicaid, are also major thoroughfares that enter our local public welfare system. Imagine in our experiment what happens to the people traveling our highway system if large numbers of entrances are blocked and lanes closed and people have to find alternative routes to independence and self-sufficiency. What if there were no more Medicaid or no more Food Stamps? Murray asks us to imagine that. In a theoretical world, beneficiaries of those programs might fend for themselves with the help of friends and family, or they might find a high paying job so as not to need help, and they may even flourish because the hardship stimulated action toward self betterment. But in the real world of community social services, people with real and often complicated needs show up wherever they can get help. Needs in reality are not as cut-and-dried as they are in the think-tanks. Not only do people suffer when programs get cut, but so does the system of linking agencies. Increased demand for services without corresponding resources causes the same kind of bottleneck experienced when there is an accident or construction on a highway. The volume of traffic does not dwindle because of road construction or an accident—it may go elsewhere—but just as an unaddressed social problem leads to other problems, the diverted traffic will eventually stack up somewhere else.

Even though social problems can be explained simply by politicians or the press, they are usually as complex and interrelated as a well-planned set of roadways that runs in and out of a major city. Yet, in practice, the actual attempts to solve major social problems are usually narrow and disconnected, much like the way our new welfare reform policy is unfolding. It is extremely difficult to coordinate the system of services in the United States because some programs are legislated, like the ones in the *Public* category in the framework above, and some are voluntary, as in the *Congregational* category. Some, like the new welfare reform system, are interlaced with three layers of government. Quite often for programs to work, they need to be supported by the private or for profit system of services through grants and contracts, or, as the data shows in chapter 4, by voluntary assistance. The road work is neither smooth nor connected. Some public agencies are under federal auspices; some are under state control; some private nonprofit agencies have parts of their budgets coming from federal, state, and local authorities, while other agency budgets in the framework are from strictly private sources.

If we step back from our experiment and try to imagine what this national public hodgepodge might look like if we were in a satellite, and then instantly be able to zoom in at the local traffic, we would see that besides the array of federal programs under siege but still intact, there are 50 states, each with a Department of Human Resources which oversees state mandated services and also administers federal block grant programs. Many of those states wanted control of welfare but had to make considerable adjustments when they actually received full control. There are 3,043 counties, most with Public Health, Mental Health, and Social Services divisions in their governmental structure. Each division has subdivisions that carry out state, federal, and/or locally mandated programs. All of those systems with their vast networks of employees and clients are adjusting to the policy changes. There are 19,279 cities (Shotzberger 1996), the larger ones having their own social service, community development and housing departments, and all are struggling to solve the social problems seen elsewhere.

The Reagan budget cuts put large volumes of traffic onto the secondary roads that constitute *the very system that now is being asked to handle the next round of cuts even more extensively than it was asked to handle the cuts of the 1980s.* These public agencies went through a transformation in the Reagan years leaving them in a scramble at the community level for leadership in service development. Even though the public entities still had the most revenue and largest numbers of clients throughout the Reagan era, they no longer held the authority they once had, nor could they presume they had the same level of revenue from year to year. Imagine a major highway leading into a large city under long-term repair. Consequently, a large volume of people have to find alternative routes and other means of transportation. Every alternative route and other modes of transportation into the city get overtaxed. Since public agencies have never come close to providing all the social welfare services to their communities they have had to rely on the help of the other members of the system of services to get the job done. In their heyday they had money and power to lead local systems. But continued major revenue losses during the 1980s changed their roles from leaders with "money in the bank" to bureaucracies with great pressure to do more with less. For the last fifteen years, they have been *highways under construction* and the service bottlenecks, both in the public and private spheres, have reflected it. The reduction in funds in the 1980s forced their focus inward, something akin to fixing the potholes, so the backed-up traffic would not be any slower. The attrition left few planners with the energy and foresight to develop an outward vision and less fiscal authority to help the secondary service providers.

If we go back to our thought experiment again, let's now imagine the public system of services being a major roadway and the private system, including the religious and congregational service system, being the secondary roads that lead people to their destination. The authorities (politicians) in our experiment decide to steer traffic to the secondary roads, or the other categories in our framework, and tell those who care for the roads (the private nonprofit, self-help, and religious congregations) to figure out a way to handle the increased traffic. We have all been on roads under construction or have been steered off a major highway to a secondary road and found the secondary road is a mess as well. Murray does not ask in his experiment how the secondary roads are going to handle the excess traffic.

UNITED WAY

How does reduced revenue combined with increasing social problems affect those 20,000 plus public entities, their various subdivisions, and the millions of people they serve? Merely analyzing statistics does not give one a perspective on the interconnections and changes in activities in the local system. One familiar with the operation of local systems might expect the United Ways to step in and assume the planning and leadership responsibilities when the roadways get bottlenecked, but they have lost the favor of the public in recent years, and in addition some United Ways too, are having trouble coordinating efforts in their complex local systems. There are 1,600 local United Ways affiliated with United Way of America which help fund about 45,000 local nonprofit secular, and sectarian agencies. United Way allocations, however, make up only 8.7 percent of member agency budgets which means agencies are an often in the reckless, dynamic, and competitive scramble for funds. Of course, some agencies get larger shares and some smaller. For example, 45 percent of The American Red Cross agencies' budgets across the country come from United Way allocations. The following statement from a 1994 United Way report called *Setting the Strategic Direction for the United Way System: Report of the Strategic Planning Committee to the Board of Governors: Discussion Draft* (United Way 1994) captures the problems faced by the 1,600 local United Ways affiliated with United Way of America:

> There is increased frustration with the intractability of these problems, and the concern that increased expenditures have not produced meaningful results. In many cases the United Way is one of a larger number of groups unable to make substantive progress on these problems. Unable to distinguish itself from other groups, United Way has watched as communities have continued to search elsewhere for assistance.

On page one of the March 18, 1998 *Catholic Charities Advofax: A Weekly Update on Congressional Acts and Issues of Importance*, it is noted that President Clinton's 1999 budget proposed $390 million in cuts in the Title XX Social Service Block Grant. In figure 3.7, I noted the impact of 1982 reductions in Title XX funds had a bearing on the service system. What is the dif-ference now? According to the Catholic Charities report, every state now stands to lose funds that have been provided since 1974 for services to chil-dren, the elderly, and people with disabilities. Programs at risk include child protection, foster care, child care, services for developmentally disabled people, mental health, home-based delivery of meals, chore services, and protective services. The problems that have given rise to these services have not gone away by any stretch of the imagination. It is just that the financing of their management is being shifted to states and localities—the second-ary roadways in our experiment.

Once again, people at the community level will have to dig in to solve local problems with the resources they have. These communities have had to do more with less in the midst of great changes. As the United Way statement above points out, agencies unable to accomplish their missions with United Way assistance have had to turn elsewhere. I believe that the "elsewhere" here is the religious community, and except for what I have offered here, we really do not know much about the kinds of services it offers, the impact of the services, and the capacity to contribute in the future.

When Senators John Ashcroft or Dan Coats (Frame 1995), or historian Marvin Olasky (1992) imply or say outright that religious charities can lead communities to the promised land of sleek, cost effective, and efficient service systems, they have not sat down with a map. It is a wrinkled, re-drawn, crossed-out and written-over map with spidery lines of so many small roads that even a local has trouble deciphering it sometimes. It shows the interconnectedness of public systems, private systems and religious community. Our political leaders and historians should be commended for recognizing that the public and private systems are overburdened, but in terms of our experiment here, they simply recommend that more traffic should be dumped onto these roads with no plan but to declare that the road named "the religious community" can handle the increasing over-flow. Without understanding the dynamics of the whole picture, we will proceed into the future with rearview mirrors. The local system is much too complicated to merely drop down such a solution without under-standing the role religion already plays in the interconnectedness of local service delivery.

UNITED WAY/RELIGIOUS INTERCONNECTION

Let us look at several examples of the interconnection just between the secular United Way and the sectarian services in local communities. There are 717 sectarian family service agencies, such as Catholic Family Services, Lutheran Family Services, and Jewish Family Services, in communities around the country that receive United Way allocations for nonreligious service provision, while 1,273 Salvation Army Corps (churches) with community based secular programs are allocated funds making up 14 percent of the organization's budgets. Although the Salvation Army hires people who are not members of their faith to work in their various programs, I highly doubt that any major figure in the Salvation Army would say that any of its programs are secular; they would instead contend that the programs reflect an expression of its faith. A combined 1,902 YMCAs and YWCAs receive United Way funding. The funds make up 6 percent and 14 percent of their budgets respectively (United Way 1996). They too must go to the funding founts to make their programs operate effectively.

Even with United Way agencies in the picture, this portrait is still sketchy. Less than a third the nonprofit human service agencies in a given community are under the United Way umbrella. Even with the United Way support, United Way member agencies still have to go into the dwindling funding arena and compete with non-United Way agencies for the remainder of their budgets. To complicate matters, there are times when non-United Way agencies have received United Way grants to provide needed community services. As United Ways move away from its general tendency of funding specific agencies, to funding the solutions to particular problems that agencies may address through specific programs, that trend will grow, and we will see even more competition for resources (United Way 1996).

There is yet another curve in the road. Those sectarian agencies like Catholic Charities, the Salvation Army, and even congregations who receive United Way funds, often receive federal, state, and local tax money to provide an even broader range of services when the public entities are overburdened. So, when the authorities start talking about what the religious community can and cannot accomplish in the area of welfare reform or other service realms, it is likely they do not understand how the elimination of one set of services at the public level affects the delivery of service at the private and sectarian level. If by chance they do, they are often so blinded by their ideology that it is impossible to have a sober discussion about how to solve complicated social problems. If communities are going to be successful in solving, managing, or preventing the range of interconnecting problems that might plague them, they will best succeed if they first understand what their community system looks like and how it functions.

PUBLIC/RELIGIOUS INTERCONNECTION

Not only is the United Way connected to the religious system of services, but so are public agencies. As I pointed out above in some detail, the public services system constitutes a semi-interconnected set of agencies and programs, often under different or dual auspices, that at some times work together and at others function at cross purposes. The headline in the last chapter that tells of counties in North Carolina vying for control of welfare reform is the most recent example of the changing tides and interconnected support systems. The Federal government has decentralized welfare reform, giving almost complete autonomy to the states. Nevertheless, the federal government requires the states to submit their welfare plans before federal funds are released. This is not the same as in the case of education, where states have complete autonomy. In the welfare reform plan, the states have required their counties to submit plans in accordance with the state guidelines, thus giving the states authority over the counties. In North Carolina, however, twenty-one counties have been allowed to design their own welfare reform plans that do not conform to the state's plan. Figure 7.1 illustrates the point that while counties can design their own plan, they still are under the auspices of the state, which is in turn under the watchful eye of the federal government. The item is a portion of a memo that was sent to each of the counties that had, as part of its plan, involvement with the faith community. This small excerpt exemplifies the multi-tiered set of interrelationships among the various levels of government and the complexities of integrating faith-based services into governmental programs.

When we study the various levels of involvement of the faith community in service provision in relation to the vast levels of service provision of the nonprofit sector in general, and then include the provisos of this or that level

---

FIGURE 7.1

Excerpt of March 3,1998 letter to sent to counties in North Carolina whose welfare plans include the use of resources from the faith community.

Faith Community Involvement. You have indicated that you plan to use resources in the faith community for life skills training and the New Focus Program. Faith community involvement in our work with the welfare population is something we have actively sought and support. While we encourage and commend your efforts to link up and work with the faith community, it is absolutely imperative to understand that government cannot condition receipt of benefits upon religious involvement in church sponsored activities, unless it is clearly voluntary on the part of the welfare recipients. This is probably not the intent of your plan, but it is important to remember that churches must not be passing out religion along with charity unless it is being voluntarily received by welfare recipients. It is a constitutional problem of separation of church and state.

---

of government, the process becomes hard to understand, and that makes it difficult for everyone except those who have the simple and often wrong answers. As I will note again, when major changes are imposed upon any part of this system of services, the ability to deliver effective services in other service realms is often hindered. The recipients of service find the system difficult to understand, and so do the community members. But interestingly, after a while, the actors in this system learn to negotiate the sudden changes, even if they have to behave dangerously or illogically, much like drivers using the shoulders of roads as alternative routes when traffic bottlenecks on their highway system. Every time the local service system loses funds or experiences a change in the direction of some policy, the participants in the system behave similarly to the drivers whose roadways change.

NONPROFIT, NON-UNITED WAY, OR SELF-HELP

Other service providers in a community service scheme are the independent agencies that are nongovernmental, nonreligious, and *not* under the auspices of the United Way. In most localities there is a range of private nonprofit agencies not under the United Way umbrella, and there is a large number of self-help groups. The nonprofit organizations are sometimes small grassroots organizations with local connections, or sometimes they are large organizations affiliated with state or national groups. Depending on the local terrain, such agencies are not under the United Way umbrella of agencies for reasons that reflect local political concerns. Yet they interact with other parts of the system to help provide services and address problems affecting the community.

In my community, for example, the local branch of the American Lung Association is not a United Way agency. Its lack of affiliation has something to do with the local politics of having a major tobacco company in town and its making large contributions to the United Way. In the politics of local social services, big corporate contributors sometimes make sure that their giving does not work at cross purposes with their overall corporate objectives. On the other hand, The Lung Association (a non-United Way agency) works with local public health doctors and the public school system in anti-smoking campaigns aimed at youth. Such efforts ultimately serve the public and private good. There is a range of self-help organizations in any given community from which nonprofit organizations eventually evolve, and quite often use the resources of the religious community. Alcoholics Anonymous is an example of a self-help organization that is intertwined with all of the systems in the model above. It is a self-help organization with religious underpinnings, often operated out of congregational sites, and is a treatment modality used in public, private nonprofit, and for-profit substance abuse treatment schemes. One might ask what does AA have to do with retrenchment, welfare policy, government, or church relationships?

AN EXAMPLE OF DEVOLUTION OR DEVILUTION ON MAIN STREET

An example of how devolution takes form on Main Street is found in the case of First Baptist Church of Philadelphia, one of the longest continuing congregations in the city. The church has 200,000 square feet of space

which is used by numerous outside groups. They charge a small mainte-
nance fee and that sum helps the small membership keep up the building.
Because of the principle of separation of church and state, this historic
structure, which needs repair, does not receive any government funds for
refurbishing. Yet, the city of Philadelphia was short on funds and eliminated a drug and alcohol rehabilitation program to which the courts
referred petty criminals who had substance abuse problems. The courts
used First Baptist's AA and NA programs as a substitute for the municipal
rehabilitation program. In 1994, for the first time in its history, the church
had to hire a security firm to protect the facility from the vandalism that
had come about with the mandatory sentencing of petty criminals to be
rehabilitated at the church-based rehabilitation programs. By late 1994, the
number of those coming to the AA and NA Programs grew to a daily average of 500 and the population of users became more abusive and more
property was stolen or damaged. The church received no warning from the
city that it planned to close down its program which had, in effect, left the
church as the only available program in the area. The congregation explic-
itly did not want to approach the city and ask for reimbursement of any
sort. With devolution, we will witness more blurring among the roles of the
public, private, and religious sectors and corresponding debates about
whether public funds can be used to refurbish a structure that serves both
public and private functions in the name of religion. In the case of First
Baptist, why would members want to become partners with the government in a welfare reform project given the poor track record of the municipal agency in forging relationships in substance abuse treatment? The general misunderstanding of the changes affecting the public system, combined with the lack of good planning and coordination, will cause more
damage than the good the policy, in theory, is supposed to create.

CONGREGATIONS

When congregational service provision is tossed into the mix on Main
Street, the logic of the system becomes even more blurred (illustrated in the
table and figure above). Many congregations play multiple roles in this
scheme of services. They, of course, house AA programs. They also serve as

congregate meal sites for the elderly and support local shelters for the homeless, to cite other familiar examples.

While more research is emerging showing the multiple level of service provision of congregations, we have really just touched the surface. Below is an excerpt from an interview of the role congregations play in service provision. The excerpt illustrates still another level of interconnection that the religious community has with the rest of the service system. Shirley is the executive director of the local United Cerebral Palsy Association, and an affiliate of the national United Cerebral Palsy Association. Some recipients of her agency's services receive Social Security disability, or Supplemental Security Income (SSI) and they are covered under The Americans With Disabilities Act. The agency is a United Way agency, and yet her funding comes from public and private sources. As changes affect one part of the system, they cannot help but affect others. Shirley characterized the pattern of organizational interconnection with the religious community across North Carolina this way:

> We have twenty-six programs across the state [North Carolina] and I would say probably ninety percent started in church basements. It was like a launching place for us to build a center. Sometimes we paid part of [the cost of the space]. And we got volunteers from that congregation. It [the effort] usually grew to building a children's center. We got a lot of help from volunteers to help us through the church organizations. We have volunteers from congregations coming in all the time to deal with different aspects of our centers. The volunteerism is wonderful.

FOR PROFIT

Finally, in the framework of local service provision there are the for-profit providers that range from home healthcare providers to therapists. As it now stands, they play an important role in the community of services. Yet, as the system of services gets stretched, such professionals will be called on increasingly to contribute more of their expertise, time, and other resources to solve problems in their communities. They may do this through participation on boards of directors of local agencies, through their own congregational programs, or other venues such as providing in-kind service as new needs arise.

THE WHOLE SYSTEM

When we step back and look at the whole system at the community level, we see an interconnected highway system; each agency, like the individual road, has its function in the larger network care. It is essential for the architects of social policy to understand this system and avoid overstating or understating its capacity to solve, manage, and prevent the major problems that the system addresses. For the politicians and pundits to merely say that the religious community can and should address this or that problem without understanding the nature of the congregational system of services in the larger scheme of community help is off base. Table 7.2 is a framework that outlines congregational roles in the community. This framework can now serve as a way to more broadly understand the congregational role in the service scheme.

The table shows the levels of congregational involvement in the provision of social services locally. The ways they serve are broken into two broad categories: *On Premises Assistance* and *Community Outreach*. Some congregations offer services for members only such as counseling and transportation to the doctor's office or day care. Others provide services to members, and to people in the neighborhood and/or the community at large such as tutoring and after-school recreation programs. Congregations host programs run by outside agencies and self- help groups. Such programs serve their members and also the broader community for example Alcoholics and Overeaters Anonymous, and Boy Scout and Girl Scout programs. In addition, congregations serve as hosts for blood drives from the Red Cross or immunization sites for flu shots from the local public health department.
Congregations offer space, volunteers and other resources to local programs. Shepherd's Centers, which serve the elderly, are now located in more than 80 communities nationwide. Congregations create community development corporations, and other separate nonprofit organizations in order to solve a range of community problems and to be able to solicit and receive public money. Congregations increasingly have become grant-makers, and while this activity takes place on the premises of congregations, it is an effort to reach out and provide resources to community betterment projects. Congregations support agencies in the community with volunteers

Table 7.2.

Congregational Framework

Location	Whom Served	Offering	Example of Service
On premises	Members Only	Member to Member	Transport to Doctor
	Community	Members to Community	Feeding Site
		Congregation to Community	AA or Child Care site
In Community	Those in need through social service agencies	Volunteers, money supplies, etc.	Habitat for Humanity
	Community	Leadership on boards Newspaper editorials	Clergy serving on Human Relations Commission

and other resources. For example a congregation may make and deliver dinner for the residents of a local municipal night shelter on a regular basis throughout the year. The local social service department may also call on a congregation to "Adopt a Social Worker" to help his or her clients with extras like rides to doctors, clothes for the kids, and other social support (Wineburg 1996). Congregations often support agencies in the community through interlocking leadership roles where clergy have permanent spots on boards of directors of agencies, or prominent church leaders also serve on agency boards. Congregational leadership is often asked to represent the broader moral concerns of the community by serving on boards and commissions that focus on the peaceful solution to community disagreements.

WHERE DO CONGREGATIONS FIT?

Congregations play a vital role in the total scheme of the interconnecting road-work that constitutes a community's care and concern for the less fortunate. When we see their offerings overlaid on the map of the larger federal and nonprofit "highways and byways" that makeup a local system of service, it is clear that congregations are a vital line, but by no stretch of the imagination can become the major conduit for the needy as the federal government puts up its detour signs. It would be devilish to think otherwise. At the local level, on the other hand, neither public, nonprofit, nor for profit agencies offer the permanence, moral grounding, sense of stability, and social glue that congregations offer to the mixture of community services.

The challenge for politicians, clergy, academics, and other community leaders is to begin laying the groundwork neighborhood by neighborhood, in order to determine problems and available resources, and the gaps between the two. In the next chapter, I will map out some ways to start unclogging the bottlenecks created by implementing the ideas in Charles Murray's thought experiment.

CHAPTER EIGHT

Being Honest, Being Decent, Being Informed

In short, we are not self created atoms manipulating or being manipulated by objective institutions. We form institutions and they form us every time we engage in a conversation that matters, and certainly every time we act as a parent or child, student or teacher, citizen or official, in each case calling on models and metaphors for the rightness or wrongness of action. Institutions are not only constraining but also enabling. They are substantial forms through which we understand our own identity and the identity of others as we seek cooperatively to achieve a decent society.

—(Robert Bellah, *The Good Society* 1991).

We must work hard locally to help our religious institutions, our institutions of higher education, and our social welfare institutions to form decent communities.

◻

SUMMARY

Major Points of Chapter 8

1. Communities are facing the reality of having more responsibility for design and delivery of local services.

2. Local institutions can be shaped by as well as shape how their communities will respond to the changes.
3. Regardless of what politicians say, the religious institutions can and will play an important, but subsidiary role in providing concrete services.
4. They may play an important moral role as the case example that is presented points out.
5. The educational community, working with the practitioner and religious community, may provide the impetus for a new way of understanding the local system and enhancing its total effectiveness.

❑

A STEP BACK, A STEP FORWARD

In the last chapter, it was pointed out that federal, state and local governments have specifically targeted the religious community to step up its involvement in local service development. It should be clear that things are easier said than done. While the talk from Washington, some of the nation's statehouses, and political think tanks make things look easy, the reality is that those developing services get bogged down in much the same way traffic does on a busy construction-laden highway. We must study the details of program development, not the rhetoric of how the religious institutions can save the day.

Take for example Charitable Choice, or section 104 of the 1996 Personal Responsibility and Work Opportunity Act (Welfare Reform). Charitable Choice, as noted earlier, allows churches to receive government money to support social services they are operating locally. There are about 300,000 churches now eligible to request government money. Allowing new entrants into the quest for resources would be fine if the money coming into the system of care locally were on the rise. But the local system now, as in 1980s, is experiencing cuts in revenue. So the effect of Charitable Choice is to put 300,000 more competitors into the scramble for fewer dollars. There is no question who will win the battle for the increasingly slimmer pickings in the local competition for scarce resources. Initially, a few smaller churches that have visible community programs for drug abusers, ex-convicts, or provide after-school tutoring might receive funds. But no matter how nice a program is theoretically, practically speaking, we are now asking small religiously based organizations to keep two sets of books so that government money can be kept distinct from other church finances. In general, the reporting and evaluation requirements for government over the years have become tedious.

The average congregation has about 180 members, a small and quite often unsophisticated economic operation. *Charitable Choice*, over the long run, will impose on small community congregations complex application, reporting, and evaluation requirements of government grants and contracts while maintaining their separate "church only" books. Small congregations will drop out of the competitive mix for the scarce resources locally leaving only the wealthier, larger congregations in the competition. Many large congregations have already started or inspired the creation of community development corporations to compete for the funds with other nonprofits locally. Competition helps create better widgets, and I am all for it in the economic realm and even support it, with qualification, in the social service realm.

Here is the qualification. In the mid-1980s in my community of Greensboro, North Carolina we had 5,000 people waiting for public housing. In the late 1990s in this same community, good economic times, we have more than 6,000 people on the waiting list for public housing. The government cuts in housing in the 1980s had more of an effect on the system of services locally than on the worsening housing crisis. In the early 1980s Greensboro's private housing efforts for the poor were nil. Then in the mid 1980s and 1990s, Greensboro formed two religiously based housing groups, one secular nonprofit, and Habitat for Humanity. One of the sectarian housing groups folded as did the secular organization, leaving two very busy private groups. So, what has been the net effect of the competition in the nonprofit realm when the flow of public money in the partnership has been reduced? It is quite plain. **People are working privately through secular and faith-based efforts, but competing for fewer dollars, and not stemming the affordable housing shortage for the working poor.** Could it be that the competitive model of social services works at making public agencies leaner and more accountable, and may even stimulate the growth of new nonprofits, but does not reduce the problems they are supposed to solve, manage, or prevent? Based on what I have outlined so far, my best projection is that as we move deeper into this era of devolution, we will need to systematically monitor how a reduction in public funds both stimulates the response of competitive private responses, and reduces the problems locally.

Our social problems are far too intricate and expansive, and our public and private nonprofit system of services, including the current system of services offered by religious congregations, are too structured and tradition-based to expect a major redesign which would make the religious community the main providers of our country's social services. The nation's 300,000 churches, synagogues, and mosques would each have to put up $225,000 to make up for the proposed social service cuts (Shapiro, 1996). Raising those kinds funds would be extremely difficult considering that Father Fred Kammer, President of Catholic Charities USA, estimated that the average congregational budget is around $100,000 (Shapiro, 1996). If we took the total of the 300,000 congregations and increased their budgets by 125 percent we would in effect create a religious social service system that is twice the size it is now.

Would such a system be more effective in handling the range of problems that faces both the public system of services and the closely connected system of private nonprofits in any given community? This is highly doubtful. On the practical side of things there has not been any lead time in making the shift from a welfare system that was purely public to one whose "job retention" function is and in many localities will continue to be in the hands of the religious community. This dynamic change in the basic function of the congregation from subsidiary player in the local system of services to most valuable player will have many ramifications not only for the way social services get designed and delivered at the local level, but also for the broader way our local institutions behave in shaping local policies.

Such an idea does not mean that we should not do something to overhaul our present system of public and private services in our nation's localities. We should. In this new reorganization, congregations should be considered precious community resources in a pool of caring public and nonprofit organizations but not the *sole* source of salvation. It does not mean that congregations won't expand their roles and be much more active in local service design and delivery. They will. Nevertheless, when one stops to think that religious congregations first provide a gathering spot for communal worship, it is amazing how such organizations muster the energy and spirit not only to help their own members, but also to offer their facilities to the community, support community agencies, and reach out with money and service nationally and internationally. If you want to give blood, attend an AA meeting, or start a scout troop, chances are good that you will wind up at a local congregation's facility. There will be innovations and some wholesale changes in the way some congregations serve their communities. But it is unimaginable to me that a large number of these organizations will ever change their main purpose or vary from what they are doing in such a way that is unrecognizable from their current way of operating.

When future social welfare historians compare the system of the 1990s and early 2000s to the one of the 2050s, they will see dramatic differences. The local system of services will be more responsible in the era to come for solving, managing, and preventing problems. As such, the system of services itself will need new conceptualization. Instead of the traditional public, private nonprofit, for profit, and religiously based services vernacular, we will need a new language and a new way of understanding the relationships, something along the order of *a community of care*, as I have mentioned before. Just as nobody would imagine a car going anywhere without its wheels, even though the engine is its most important part, nobody in the future will imagine a local *community of care* solving, managing, or preventing problems without assistance from the religious community, even though it is not its engine.

That is a far different view of the role of religion in local services from the one I had as a VISTA Volunteer some 25 years ago and as a graduate student studying social services right after that. It is clearly a view founded on a different set of ideas about the role of religion in social services, and different from the view coming from the political arena. It is somewhat arrogant for politicians to imagine a system of public welfare headed by the religious community, without accurately assessing *what that community really is, what that community has done in the last two decades, and what that community would* **volunteer** to do in the next two decades. With such information, the resources of the religious community might fit better into the larger scheme of public, private nonprofit, and self-help operations at the local level.

So from my perch, before we enlist the assistance of the faith community in contributing to the solution of community problems, every prospective congregation ought to be **asked** whether it wants to participate, assessed as to its capability of doing what is asked, reviewed for what kind of practical support it has to offer, and queried as to whether a requirement for such support would hinge on the recipient adhering to religion in general or a brand of religion in particular. Such an assessment would give a far clearer picture of whether congregations want to participate, and just what resources congregations can and cannot offer. The information gleaned from such an assessment could provide some sobering guidance for community planners and help solidify the voluntary aspect of congregational participation.

If politicians continue to reduce funding for public sector services and also try to meet the current demands with only religious resources, social services offered from the religious community will have to expand exponentially. The religious community does not have the capability or capacity to do that. With extreme pressure from the government on these voluntary organizations, either subtly or directly, to do something beyond their missions they will no longer be voluntary organizations. As noted in the last chapter, First Baptist Church in Philadelphia had to hire a security officer to stem the vandalism that resulted when the court, without conferring with church officials, started requiring petty criminals to participate in one of the many Alcoholics Anonymous groups the church houses. The church pays the cost of the security (personal visit, May 1995). This is not an isolated case either. A pastor with whom I also spoke told me that the same thing happened to him in a parish in Syracuse, New York. As governments cut their programs, they could create much more local harmony, and lay the groundwork for better programming through politeness and collaboration with congregations and other voluntary organizations in mapping strategies to solve some complicated problems.

The support that religious congregations can lend to local social services is attractive because they are small and less bureaucratic than government agencies and can solve problems and meet needs immediately. The spirit underscoring their effectiveness comes in part because at this point their efforts are voluntary. Compelling them to hire security by cutting programs and forcing people to their doorsteps, or targeting them from the political podium with religious programs introduced by the government as in Mississippi, or North Carolina, will not create the type of system of local services that everyone would like: one that is willing, humane, responsive, and cost-effective. Existing primarily as places for voluntary worship, religious communities will be most effective in delivering the services that express their faith. It is quite dangerous for politicians to try to force congregations to expand beyond what they feel designed to do or what they are capable of doing. If politicians try that too long, the government will become the moral hostage of an institution that has had the market on the moral metaphor much longer than the political institution.

WHAT IS NEXT

Here is a case that I believe symbolizes things to come. The headline of an editorial in the July 9, 1995 edition of the *Utica Observer Dispatch*, a small upstate New York newspaper, stated "We must finally give a damn." The editorial page editor, Tim Chavez, asks a rhetorical question: "Why is a suburban pastor vigorously opposing with pulpit and petition a $150,000 state grant politically proffered for an isolated 25 member private hunting club in the Adirondack mountains just a few miles from Utica?" The story is about challenging, with pen and pulpit, the time-tested practice of pork barrel spending. Reverend John Holt, leader of First United Methodist Church of New Hartford, New York, a suburb of Utica did so simply on moral grounds.

He and 150 parishioners sent a petition to Republican Governor George Pataki of New York, a spending reformer, and William Sears, the Republican state senator who sponsored the pork project under attack, asking them to rescind the project and use the money on something that affects more people. Pataki did not respond, and Sears's response was legalistic and calculated. He said the grant was legal, and he helped his constituents. Sears's response was in the spirit of the literal meaning of pork barrel spending, which means "to bring home the bacon" to one's immediate constituents. The real meaning is all too familiar: I will do whatever it takes to keep me in office. Reverend Holt's challenge was important mostly because it gave a voice to the poor and disaffected. More mainline pastors will do that in the future.

The article is also important because a local mainline cleric held a legislator accountable for his spending actions on moral grounds, and challenged the legislator's narrow and legalistic interpretation of his spending actions. Reverend Holt drew the battle lines in terms of fairness, honesty, right and wrong. While Holt may have lost this moral battle to legalistic and situational values that underpin pork spending, he will ultimately win the war of establishing a broader set of community values that will form the foundation of policies to come. He won't do that alone, either.

THINGS TO COME

As more congregations have a stake in the welfare of their communities and become partners in providing for that welfare, they will educate themselves and they will challenge policy decisions on moral grounds. This may be so especially in cases where politicians attempt to make local religious congregations and agencies the domain for designing and delivering social services in the name of efficiency, and then spend money on their cronies. Congregations will increasingly form partnerships with local agencies, both public and private, in addressing social concerns. Those on the front lines will demand the type of honesty people expect from their partners in business or marriage. Over time, communities will stake out a set of values that reflect those of the mainline religious congregations because they have the longstanding track record of involvement in local service provision.

This story is also meaningful beyond one upstate New York community because another dimension of its moral implications stands out. Holt believed that New York State needed to cut its wasteful spending. What surprised me was that there was not a tinge of politics in Holt's challenge. New Hartford is traditionally a Republican haven. While Reverend Holt is now an independent, he told me that he is from a Republican family, and he was always a Republican. Reverend Holt demanded honesty. And while there seems to be various brands of honesty these days, it was refreshing to see it being demanded from a Republican legislator by a preacher with Republican bloodlines. Reverend Holt's congregation offers numerous programs to his congregants, to the broader community, and it supports the efforts of agencies in the surrounding region as well. Reverend Holt himself serves on the board of two agencies that provide critical support services for children and families, and he is also active in a project that addresses the effects of racism. Trying to shape the moral environment. Holt said:

> We need to concentrate on the places where the most people can be helped—particularly education and agencies working with people in need. To see resources used for things more of an entertainment orientation (25 member hunting club) when needs are not being met for so many in need is something that is not just, but borders on immoral. This (petition) comes not as a condemnation of any particular project, but as more of a concern in this day and age of very limited resources, that we need to be careful where we spend.

We have become so used to lying, cheating, and stealing in politics that truth is no longer a real standard that we use to judge our politicians. Consequently, far too few people of moral authority, whether they are clergy or not, have had the courage to stand up and publicly challenge fraudulent policy choices. Truth has taken a back seat to party loyalty on both sides of the aisle. As congregations continue to distribute more resources and become closer to being equal partners in the community of care, we will probably see more Reverend Holts and possibly protest marches like the one in Greensboro. As politicians make demands on the religious community, either in the abstract, or in practice, those same politicians can expect to be held to much greater moral accountability.

NEW VALUES

Eventually, communities will need to discuss comprehensive community planning, sketching out what they want their local social service system to look like, and more importantly, the values that will make their communities decent places to live. Currently, local systems are nothing more than an array of public, private, and religious agencies and organizations— some bureaucratic and hamstrung by layers of statutes, others well-lubricated and doing their jobs. Some are slowed by a lack of funding or leadership, and still others are involved in causes on a purely voluntary basis regardless of community need. By and large, it is an increasingly decentralized system with a purpose few can define or interpret. That is why it is easy to attack.

Nevertheless, the system is held together by people who are often underpaid, or overworked volunteers, but people who share a set of values to mend or change some of the most horrible human conditions imaginable. They continue their work despite budget cuts and assaults on their honest efforts by the uninformed. In reality, they are involved in some of the most soul wrenching and difficult work possible. To preserve this spirit in the next era, we need to *reinvent the local service system* so that everyone understands its purpose and function. It has to be seen as a system where human beings—professionals, volunteers, young, old, and in-between—work to build safe, caring, lively, and spirited communities. If the return to local service design and delivery is going to have any chance of working, there has to be a general consensus on some basic values underpinning the system of local care.

Reverend Holt hit on the first of three. (1) *Being Honest.* The religious community *cannot* take over the social services in this country, and politicians must be honest about that. The religious community can be partners in a more localized community of care and they could play a greater role in carving a moral framework for its operations. While there might be competing moral frameworks, there is common ground. (2) *Being Decent*. The religious community can ensure that no child goes to bed hungry if there is enough food in the community; nobody sleeps in the street if there is enough shelter in the community; not a soul is turned away from medical care if there is enough medical care in the community; and not one person dies of the cold when there is enough heat in the community. The religious community, especially the mainline religious community that has quietly been delivering services since nationhood, must become more public-minded in trying to shape its vision of a public morality. It is one thing to win the political favors of the religious right with the rhetoric of cutbacks, efficiency in government, and promoting the idea of a religious takeover of social services. It is quite another to support cuts to the poor and then dole out $150,000 to members of a private hunting club as in the Reverend Holt episode. (3) *Being Informed*. Mainline denominations could serve the public well by regularly and systematically providing educational forums to inform congregants and the broader community about the range of issues facing the community. This is already happening in some communities but will have to expand.

WHERE ARE WE AND WHAT CAN BE DONE?

Right now, we are in the early stages of a new policy era when local systems of care are going through stages of refinement and redevelopment. It is very difficult to decipher how larger policy decisions like the Reagan budget cuts of the 1980s or the new welfare reform of the 1990s affect the operation of local service systems. It is also hard to discern just how social policy develops locally as religious institutions, whose members are also citizens, become more knowledgeable about the scope of the problems in the community. Communities will continue to gain an increased knowledge of both the complexities and solutions of social problems. As we move into a more mature era, communities will understand what can and cannot be accomplished privately, and what should be accomplished through a combination of well-planned public and private efforts. Such a process will evolve but it can be stimulated with a more *conscious* interplay of government, the religious community, educational institutions, and the nonprofit sector including the foundations.

PRACTICAL SUGGESTIONS FOR THE
ACADEMIC COMMUNITY

The academic community can be essential in the development of new local service configurations. In chapter 2, I listed ten areas of research that the academic community could undertake to broaden the knowledge the we have about the intersection of policy, religion, and local social services. Those ten areas are displayed in figure 8.1. If we are really serious about finding workable solutions to solving, managing, and preventing major social problems, it is essential to focus on understanding the actors in the system of services that make up the community of care, and it is important to understand the interaction among the providers in the system in order to develop policies and services that allow indigenous service systems to function at their peek effectiveness.

1. Understanding Emerging and Historical Partnerships at the
Local Level Between the Religious Community and Social
Service Providers

With this knowledge, we can have more effective policy debates and discussions that would lead to service development based on the documented strengths of the local system instead of ideological thinking that results in policies that weaken instead of strengthens local services.

2. Learning More about the Capacity of Congregations and
Faith-based Charities to Handle More Service Responsibilities
and Building Those Capacities

The research about historical partnerships and congregational-agency relationships would logically lead to an understanding of the services congregations are providing and their relationships with sectarian charities that might be connected to the denomination. After such a study, we can begin to discuss what congregations can do in the future.

3. Deciphering the Process by Which Faith-based Organizations Choose to Become Involved in Volunteering and Providing Other Resources for Community Projects

Understanding of how these indigenous organizations operate together and developing more effective and creative ways to draw them into the service delivery mix would strengthen their organizations and the community as well as services.

FIGURE 8.1

Ten Areas of Research

1. Understanding emerging and historical partnerships at the local level between the religious community and social service providers.
2. Learning more about the capacity of congregations and faith-based charities to handle more service responsibilities and building those capacities.
3. Deciphering the process by which faith-based organizations choose to become involved in volunteering and providing other resources for community projects.
4. Evaluating the effectiveness of involvement in community projects, for both the client, faith-based organization, other members of the partnership, and the local community.
5. Determining outcomes—whether the effort solved, managed, or prevented the problems it was designed to tackle.
6. Understanding and delineating the roles and functions of faith-based congregations.
7. Determining training requirements.
8. Measuring costs of service and contributions of volunteers and other in-kind resources.
9. Understanding how the interaction of these efforts noted above contribute to local policy development.
10. Comparing different communities in order to develop new and testable policy theory.

---

4. Evaluating the Effectiveness of Involvement in Community Projects, for Both the Client, Faith-based Organization, Other Members of the Partnership, and the Local Community

The nonprofit and faith-based community would serve themselves to link up with universities, colleges, and community colleges in their localities to develop systems of evaluation for the projects that are in operation. They all profess a mission to serve the community and this would be an opportunity to form partnerships to do just that. Funding agencies and policymakers appreciate good evaluative efforts.

5. Determining Outcomes—Whether the Effort Solved, Managed, or Prevented the Problems Designed to Tackle.

Right with evaluation is the development of standards or outcome measures which a program or partnership should strive to achieve. The benefits include a continual flow of concrete information on what works and what does not; determining ways to do things better or developing a rationale for continuation of specific operations; development of a community database and workable solutions to specific problems.

6. Understanding and Delineating the Roles and Functions of Faith-based Congregations

Using the evaluation and developing yardsticks for success, we can start to be much more specific about who should provide what type of services to the partnership at the community level, especially with scarce resources.

7. Determining Training Requirements

Once there is some understanding of who provides what services best, training needs can be assessed.

8. Measuring Costs of Service and Contributions of Volunteers and Other In-kind Resources

Training costs can be assessed for people working in various roles in building community partnerships.

9. Understanding How the Interaction of These Efforts Noted Above Contribute to Local Policy Development

The specific kind of research I have noted in the eight points outlined provides a solid foundation upon which to understand the operation of the local system of services and the realities that are created when the intersection of policy, religion, and service are joined at the community level.

10. Comparing Different Communities in Order to Develop New and Testable Policy Theory

This type of comparison is essential for a wider understanding of what works and what does not work. There may be times when a community decides to end a project, or not even start one, while another community has ironed out the same problems. Such comparisons across communities will assist in understanding program development, strengthening partnerships, and providing data for larger policy debate and discussion. When these ten things are in place, we will start to have an overarching framework and a common language in which to talk about these issues.

WHAT WE NEED TO KNOW FROM THE PRACTITIONERS

It becomes clear that if the academic community takes up the ten concerns that I outlined above, there will be a far greater understanding of the relationship among the participants in the local scheme of services. It is hoped that this could lead to knowing how to build successful programs locally. Still there is a wealth of knowledge that resides in the practice arena that has to be brought to the attention of the public for a greater understanding of how the organizations in the local system operate independently and in cooperation with other organizations at the community level. From the practice world, communities need the following things:

A Community Understanding

Every community has a system of services that to the average community resident might appear incomprehensible and overwhelming. As communities take on more of the responsibilities for financing the solutions to local problems, they will need ways to educate the public about the range of problems, the nature of the organizations that are trying to solve and manage them, and what is needed to be successful. Organizations need to develop internal ways of educating the public. They might want to have a slot on their boards for at least one media expert, who can bring a "media mentality" to the leadership level of the organization. In addition, communities need to build coalitions for the purpose of educating the public about interconnected problems. For example, there is a connection between the lack of reading ability and youth crime, and a deeper connection when we understand that the mom who comes off welfare cannot find decent housing and has to go to a shelter, go to her job, change schools for her kids, and the kids fall behind in their ability to read. The practitioner is best equipped to help the community see the connections among housing, welfare, crime, and children's school performance.

Many communities have access to the public cable TV stations where agencies, if they wanted, could come together to educate the community. Quite obviously, they would be better off if they could work with the academic community and support their educational efforts with good data. Along those lines, the facilities of larger religious institutions could serve as community-based centers for educational efforts that are designed to help communities more keenly understand local efforts to address their problems.

Keep Records and Stories

The community, for example, will want to know the number of children who need health care coverage, who could use reading assistance, or would like a big brother or sister. As was pointed out in chapter 4, if cannot be counted it doesn't count. That kind of thinking appeals to the bookkeeper in many of us. On the other hand, we need the stories of what hides behind the facts and figures so that we can be reminded of our humanity. Good record keeping with an eye toward using it to broaden the greater community's understanding of particular and interconnected concerns is something to work toward accomplishing.

Sharing Information and Program Ideas

The local community will have to find ways of using the available technology to its fullest potential. What most people who have not been involved in human services do not understand is that the system of services is not a socialistic entity where organizations receive according to their need and ability. There is a built-in competitive mentality because there is always less money than there are needs to be addressed. In a for-profit world, the Chamber of Commerce and the Better Business Bureau set up voluntary membership organizations systems to ensure that the competition is done fairly. It is common to see a McDonalds, Wendys, and a Burger King right next to each other selling hamburgers. They create a hamburger culture and the competition supposedly creates a better hamburger.

A new arm, or at least a new function, must be added to the community human services network, one that steers the community away from autonomous pursuits toward unified service. At one time, the United Way may have served this function, at another, universities or colleges. Now it is important for communities to find ways to meet the complicated challenges of the next century. Maybe United Ways, colleges, universities, and public agencies could work together to develop such mechanisms. The name of such a vehicle is not as important as its function: it might be called an institute, a consortium, or a center. Through it, human-services participants—directors, providers, volunteers, recipients—who give the service network its character and life can explore ways to reshape the community system. Such entities could provide a forum to identify promising practices and encourage their visibility and exchange.

Instead of public money and private sector initiatives funding the solution of isolated problems in partial ways, funds for these new arms or service functions are devoted to unification of the community services system and education of the public. At a human services center, the participants could share experiences, explore new approaches to service design and delivery, and learn new service technologies. More importantly, a center of this kind would be devoted to the betterment of the whole system.

A community service center would facilitate technologically advanced needs assessments. Professional development workshops for agency staff would help them update skills in particular areas. The center also would

allow directors or providers to debate complicated matters in an open setting. Conferences featuring experts from different service areas would be an
ongoing aspect of such a center. The possibilities are endless, and the
prospect of unifying a fragmented system is realistic and exciting.

The Offerings of the Religious Community

If such a such a center were in place at the community level, congregations
would be able to assess how they are contributing to the solutions to local
problems and just what they may be able to contribute in the future. On the
one hand, they would be able to let others know how they express their faith
through community service, give details of the kinds of activities their volunteers participate in, and show the ways their facilities are being used. For
those congregations that don't keep records, this might be the ideal stimulus to start. Through such activities the religious community could move
into a new era of service development at the community level and add even
another dimension to the principle of Community Samaritanship noted
earlier.

This level of Community Samaritanship would bring the religious
providers to the larger community planning table. Each congregation or
faith community would have an added role in their being a Community
Samaritan. They would continue their range of assistance as discussed in
chapter 4, providing volunteers, space, and money to community agencies,
as well as offer the range of social service programs they provide to their
members and neighbors. But in their new role as Community Samaritans
the faith community could offer a new moral dimension to the local system
through which the broader community acts toward its needy. (Right now
moral leadership is rarely found at the community level and if it is offered,
it is ad hoc. Part of this is due to the to the complicated road work I outlined
in the last chapter). When an aspect of policy is flawed and hurts a person
it is supposed to help, the Community Samaritans would be responsible for
alerting the public to the moral problems posed by the policy.

Let us look at a hypothetical case. A mother wants to work, or is working, but childcare subsidies run out. Now she cannot work because she has
no place for her child. As it stands currently, this is not a moral issue but a
private one between the woman, her employer, and those who subsidize
childcare. The Community Samaritans may, in fact, be able to find the sort

of child care support which they did in the previous scheme of service delivery. They will be expected to continue this in the future. But in their new role as Community Samaritans, they also take on the responsibility of outlining moral problems in policies. In this case, working at low wages makes it difficult for a woman to both work and tend to her children. As such, Community Samaritans lay the moral basis for policy change.

Of course, the Community Samaritan concept will not be able to work unless the educational institution brings its technical expertise to the community planning table. The nonprofit and public providers will have to set up a mechanism like a chamber of commerce which provides an environment where effective services can unfold, and then the religious community can bring its brand of rationality to a busy road system and promote the larger concept of morally based community partnerships.

CHAPTER NINE

Some Evolving Partnerships in a Changing Environment

"Do we have the capacity to take on this job description? Is any extra money coming to us to do this extra work? Do we want to? How do we know what to do if we do want to get involved? Who knows what the churches in my town are doing already to help those in need? We don't know who's doing what. Or is our job mainly to save people's souls and tend to our congregation's needs? Should we get political? Who says our services are necessarily better than those at County Mental Health or the school lunch program? We all wanted to fix the welfare system, but don't want to see people going homeless. WHAT SHOULD WE DO?"

(North Carolina Council of Churches).

"When I am a mother, I will never let my kids go hungry."

—Hannah Wineburg, age 12.

◨

MAIN POINTS OF CHAPTER 9

In this chapter I plan to describe three efforts of building partnerships between the faith community and the local service systems as the efforts relate to the New Welfare Reform. My focus will be on North Carolina, but the special appendix at the end of the chapter lists, and in some instances describes, other efforts elsewhere in the country. Reports and articles related to welfare reform and names of contact people are listed. Those listed may be outdated by press time and there may be many new ones as well.

❏

Welfare reform of this era has both similarities and differences from that of the Reagan period. As I have noted, the major difference is that the communities will have to do much more to keep women in their jobs than they did in the Reagan era because once these women reach their time limits for assistance they are no longer entitled to public help. In North Carolina, the state provides the funds for women on assistance for two years initially, after which she must be off assistance for three years before she is eligible to receive the remaining three years of aid. When she has received a total of five years of assistance, she is *ineligible for* federal assistance. In North Carolina, the first wave of recipients who met the two-year deadline occurred in August of 1998. This means quite a bit to local communities especially if times are rough economically, or a major problem like the lack of affordable child care or transportation, which inhibits productive employment.

In addition, as the news article shown in figure 9.1 indicates, cuts in federal dollars and a "hold the line" local budget approach, forces the system of services to change. What lies beneath the following descriptions of local efforts to cope with the changes are the numerous meetings, discussions, presentations, grant proposals, and news articles. There is a tone of hope and sometimes frustration, at least in the Jubilee material, that welfare reform is unfair, yet at the same time there is an acknowledgment that it is imminent and must be dealt with as quickly and effectively as possible.

What follows are descriptions of three different efforts in North Carolina designed in some way to handle the vast changes that are occurring at intersection of welfare reform policy, social services, and the religious community. Few have paid attention to how the Reagan cuts continue to alter behavior, often confuse the actors in service development, and change the delivery system locally, without significantly resolving the problems the policies are supposed to remedy. What follows are examples of the fetal stages of program development in three organizations. The first organization, the North Carolina Council of Churches is a statewide education and advocacy group. Its Jubilee project, which is concerned with welfare reform, started officially with paid staff in late 1997. Unofficially, the program had been in operation on a volunteer basis for almost a year prior to that.

Next, I will describe The Welfare Reform Liaison Project emerging out of Mt. Zion Baptist Church in Greensboro, North Carolina. As I have noted,

FIGURE 9.1

The Story So Far

This April 1998 news article brings to light the ideas presented here.

Triad

B

Budget cuts target day care

⬤ Parents protest the elimination of a day care for mentally handicapped children.

BY RICH MCKAY
Staff Writer

Azell Reeves' son Timothy is severely mentally handicapped. He's 8 years old. Can't walk. Can't operate his wheelchair and isn't potty-trained.

He can't be left alone, and no regular day care center will take him, Reeves said. She knows, she's tried. She found her godsend in the county's before-and-after school Friends Program and its daylong summer Friends Program that serves as a day care for mentally handicapped children at the Kendall Center.

As of July 1, the new budget year, the Friends Program will be cut to save the county's Mental Health Department $132,-000. It's part of $1.3 million in proposed cuts forced by shrinking federal dollars and orders from the Guilford County Board of Commissioners to hold the line on the department's current budget.

The cuts will leave Timothy and nearly two dozen other children with no place to go.

Along with the day care program goes the Beacon Center's clubhouse in High Point, which served as a center for mentally handicapped adults; reduced respite programs; and jobs left vacant to save money.

Reeves joined more than a dozen parents who pleaded, protested and even begged against the cuts at the Tuesday night meeting of the Guilford County Area Mental Health, Developmental Disabilities and Substance Abuse Board.

"We're working families," she told the board. "You want us to go on welfare?" She explained that she and many other parents would have to quit their jobs to take care of their children.

"Either way it will cost," Reeves said. "Get real. We need help. It's up to you."

Bert Davis Jr., the board's chairman, said there was nothing they could do about the cuts right now. The board has its instructions from the county commissioners, who control the purse strings.

But the board agreed to set up a task force that would look for ways to work with the community and look for private

Please see **MENTAL,** *Page* **B2**

the growth of poverty and the problems facing the elderly and working poor from the Reagan and Bush years straight through the good economic times of the Clinton years had already affected local services. Due to cutbacks in other programs, Mt. Zion distributed $379,000 to help people with food, rent, transportation, prescription drugs, child care, and the like from 1988 to 1997, the nine years the church kept statistics. That takes into account neither the numerous onsite programs the church offered, nor the countless volunteer hours used to administer such programs. That's just the just cash outlay.

Surprisingly, *seventy-five percent* of the people who received help were not members of Mt Zion. Those demands increased throughout the Reagan years, but the church only started keeping records in 1988. The senior pastor of the church, and an associate minister in charge of the Welfare Reform Liaison Project, knew that the new welfare reform would increase the demands on their congregation. In 1988, the church started obeying the first law of program development: if it can't be counted, the accountant doesn't count it. Thus, in 1997, they decided after a good look at their data, to develop a nonprofit corporation to handle, in a systematic way, what they anticipated would be extraordinary demands on their church. A major reason for developing the nonprofit corporation was to be able to garner wider support from the community financially and with other resources than if they remained a church program.

Here is an example how welfare reform operates locally. Guilford County's welfare reform plan, which had to be submitted to the State of North Carolina, calls for closer ties with the religious community. The second priority recommendation in category number 3 on page 16 of the plan—**Staying Off Welfare After Going To Work**—seeks to "Recruit civic organizations, *faith communities [my emphasis]*, and service organizations to serve as mentors to Work First (North Carolina's welfare program) participants." Mt. Zion has been pro-active in getting a jump on what will undoubtedly be a substantial change for the religious community in Greensboro.

The third welfare reform effort started shortly after the Jubilee project and the Welfare Reform Liaison Project. Nevertheless, the Faith Matters project gives form to some of the statistics used earlier, in that the story behind the effort is far more complex. Here, the woman starting the program was a member of Guilford County's welfare reform planning committee. Realizing that something had to be done to help working poor women from falling back into welfare because of lack of transportation, adequate child care, or life skills needed to cope with the difficulties of trying to make it, she thought she would start a one-to-one mentoring program that would serve two purposes: (1) " to provide avenues of ministry for women of faith who are active in their church/synagogue/mosque members looking for new ways to do mission work"; and (2) provide one-to one mentoring "to help economically disadvantaged women (mentees) improve themselves spiritually, psychologically, economically and educationally." (Faith Matters Document 1998). Collectively, the three programs give a snapshot of the activities happening all over.

After the program descriptions of Jubilee, The Welfare Reform Liaison Project, and Faith Matters, is an appendix which lists other partnerships, reports, articles, and names and addresses of other projects around the country. This list is not complete but was included to illustrate how the shift in policy has stimulated much activity.

As I present these programs, it is important to keep in mind that the leaders of these efforts understand that passing welfare back to the local communities has meant pressure for congregations and other types of faith-based organizations to make a coherent and organized response to something that is in fact vague, amorphous, and confusing. As I talked and worked with each, I found their efforts were grounded in an almost unexplainable care and concern for the women and children affected by this policy. Nevertheless, each knows that the religious community is confused, as are the social service community, the recipients of service, and politicians.

All of the leaders of the programs I will describe have been to numerous meetings, have been on statewide and local welfare reform planning committees, have attended numerous conferences and workshops, and have read extensively about this new policy and its intended and unintended consequences for localities. In effect, they are the public academics in that they are *teaching their communities* about this policy and *planning action* as well. In the confusion, each is clear that something must be done to buffer the shock to women and children, and also to educate the community about the flaws in the policy so that somewhere, somehow, changes can be made. *They, like my daughter, will not let the children of their community go hungry.*

JUBILEE

One effort that helps to *educate* North Carolina congregations and *make them more effective* as they enter the public square in their communities is the Jubilee project of the North Carolina Council of Churches.

As an ecumenical set of denominations working for social justice in North Carolina since the 1930s, the NC Council of Churches has long worked on issues of poverty and public welfare. In 1997, they launched a Special Project, called JUBILEE, to educate and organize various faith groups across the state on welfare reform. A planning document reveals that its ultimate purpose "is to bring a justice-focused moral vision to the welfare and employment policy debate." This will happen "by building the capacity of faith groups to understand welfare policy and speak for themselves about families, work, and welfare needs." (JUBILEE 1997)

Here's what JUBILEE has done. Over the past two years, they have made presentations on welfare and what people of faith can do for ministries with families, as well as advocacy, to more than 100 forums. These include congregations, denominational conferences, and workshops in conventions such as those for county social services directors and staff. In two pilot counties, JUBILEE has helped organize an interracial, ecumenical group of clergy and lay leaders and brought them into a formal collaboration with the county department of social services.

These kinds of partnerships are also being fostered in counties across the state. What might be kept in mind for the future is not only that communities will have to work with the issue of welfare and work, but also that race and diversity concerns will undoubtedly emerge as different congregations work together.

The goal of these new arrangements is to set up a mechanism for enlisting congregational assistance for families moving from welfare to work. As I noted earlier, welfare reform is about job retention so emerging programs from congregations will have some kind of assistance that keeps people employed. In each pilot county, and also in twelve others as of summer 1999, a new coordinator for Church-Work First (North Carolina's Welfare Program) collaboration has been installed. Called Faith Community Coordinators, and modeled after the first such coordinator in the Charlotte, North Carolina (see figure 6.3) social services office, these persons keep the ball rolling in enlisting congregations to provide transportation, mentoring, long-term partnerships, and other help with families who choose this kind of backup. In the two pilot counties, JUBILEE has refined a program to match "faith teams" in congregations with willing Work First families. Families First originated in a county crisis assistance ministry program, and JUBILEE refined it and made it into a replicable program, with a train-the-trainers manual.

The Families First model is one where a social services "link person," generally the Faith Community Coordinator where these exist, trains local faith teams to enter into a one-year covenant relationship of support and mutual learning with a family leaving welfare. JUBILEE has learned that congregations need adequate orientation, continuing support, and training if these matches are going to be done in a respectful and effective way. In the pilot counties and in communities with Faith Community Coordinators in place, a growing number of matches are helping both church members and families learn more about what it takes to deal with overcoming poverty and achieving more economic stability.

While JUBILEE does this kind of organizing to find volunteers for families losing welfare benefits, they also take a critical look at the new welfare laws and call attention to the need for structural systems change. They ask questions about whether indeed the faith community can provide all the assistance families need as billions are withdrawn from the public safety net. Through surveys in the two pilot counties, they are assessing what congregations think about their capacity to step in where welfare policy designers hope they will.

JUBILEE links people in congregations with the policy organizations that can better lobby for worker-friendly policies like promotion of a wage that can sustain a family's independence, health care coverage for all people, (one out of seven North Carolinians is uninsured), and more funding for child care and public transit. JUBILEE challenges the state's anti-labor union stance by providing a theological framework for examining the wisdom of a welfare policy that defines the problem as workers' laziness, rather than an economic arrangement in which about 20 percent of the state's workers earn below poverty level wages. JUBILEE is trying to add some balance the public discourse.

JUBILEE is moving into a new component called VOICES of EXPERI-ENCE. This will be a qualitative evaluation of welfare from the voices of those families who are in the Work First program or have recently gone off. VOICES of EXPERIENCE will explore: What is life like now for them? What works, and what does not? How should the welfare policies be changed to truly enable one to move up and out? Most evaluations paid for by the state are quantitative and are concerned with how many months the client stayed on the new job or how many clients returned to the welfare rolls after going to work.

VOICES will also bring together five grassroots groups comprised of welfare parents and their advocates and allies: Southerners for Economic Justice, Welfare Reform Liaison Project (see next group featured), the NC Family Leadership Development Initiative (mothers in the social services system), and A Healing Place social justice and healing ministry. They will learn each other's perspectives and cross-train skills. Advocates will show families how they can testify at the county commissioners meeting for a better local welfare plan. Faith-based job training leaders will show advocates and parents how they weave faith and hope into workplace preparation and community organizing. JUBILEE"s goal is to magnify the voice of these people who directly experience the polices designed for them by others, by people who generally have not walked in their shoes.

One finding of JUBILEE—not surprising—is that people in congregations are often eager to help families one-on-one. There is far less of an inclination to look at the big picture of how our state and nation treats working families, and to work for such things as family wage and health insurance for all people. Still, as JUBILEE continues to tend to the emergency needs of families who must lose benefits and try to survive on low wages, they maintain their original question: Is welfare reform fair? They work to cultivate a body of the faithful who are not only helpers, but challengers.

WELFARE REFORM LIAISON PROJECT

In the first paragraph of the Mt. Zion Church statement that justifies the need for their program, it is noted that "in the last nine years at Mt Zion Baptist Church Inc., we have distributed over $379,789 to help families avoid eviction from their houses, help elderly people pay for much needed prescriptions, and help other families keep electricity." The second paragraph illustrates why Mt. Zion had to do something to prepare for the new welfare reform: "Strikingly, over the last six years, *75 percent of the help went to people who were not members of Mt. Zion.* Many of these individuals were referred to Mt, Zion from other local community agencies such as: The Department of Social Services Emergency Assistance Program, Project Independence, Community Action, Urban Ministry, Work First and Greensboro Housing Coalition, to name a few programs." The goals of the Welfare Reform Liaison Project as stated in its organizational plan are:

a. To raise and distribute funds to the needy;
b. To help connect people to resources in the community and the church if they desire;
c. To help teach congregants from Mt. Zion and other congregations within the community how to minister to the needs of the poor in ways that are most effective, given the capacity and resources of the congregation;
d. To provide understandable, useful breakdowns on welfare policy changes, their context and projected long term effects for the faith community. (Welfare Reform Liaison Project, 1997).

In the years since Welfare Reform Liaison Project has been a nonprofit organization it has been successful in each of the goals listed above. In cooperation with the Emergency Assistance Program of Mt. Zion it has raised and distributed funds to help women with transportation, child care, and housing. It has helped people connect to resources in the community by instituting a job training program in collaboration with a local community college. It has developed a partnership with the United Way to distribute goods from the National Gifts In Kind Program. Through this effort participants have been trained in various aspects of the distribution of goods from taking inventory to shipping and have made valuable contacts in social services, education, and business networks.

After securing a grant, Welfare Reform Liaison Project held a community forum where more than 200 representatives of congregations, faith-based agencies, as well as public and private nonprofit agencies met and discussed how to better cooperate and share resources to help solve the problems facing recipients and members of the system serving them. While the leadership of the Welfare Reform Liaison Project is visionary, the true force behind the effort is the pastor of Mt. Zion who has quietly extended his church's influence to the broader community.

FAITH MATTERS

This is a new program started by a member of St. Mathews United Methodist Church. In February of 1998 "19 people from 11 different houses of worship met at St. Mathews for an orientation about Faith Matters." The specific goals of the program are the following:

> To partner on a one-to-one basis a woman who is low income or receiving Work First assistance with a woman of faith who will support and help her discover her goals in life, then help her meet those goals.
>
> Mentor and mentees will undergo extensive training. A minimum of (1) one year commitment must be agreed upon by the mentor to work in the program.
>
> The mentees must sign a covenant agreement to participate in weekly spiritual classes. These classes are ecumenical in design.
>
> Training and counseling will be customized to meet the needs of each woman]. For our pilot program, we will enroll 10 mentees. (Faith Matters document 3/98)

Strategies to achieve our goals are:

> Enable each participant/mentee to define her life goals and meet them.
>
> Facilitate the development of life skills including:
>   Communication skills
>   Conflict management skills
>   Money management
>   Parenting skills
>   Time management skills

Help each participant/mentee develop healthy [self] esteem

Network/collaborate with other community resources.

Facilitate Job search skills:
  Resume writing
  Interviewing skills
  Dress for success

Provide opportunity for participant/mentee to give back to Faith Matters through speaking about her experience, writing her story, and mentoring a program participant (Faith Matters Document 4/98)

CHARITY, JUSTICE, CARE, AND CONCERN

The three programs are examples of the kinds of efforts going on elsewhere around the country. If anything concrete can be drawn from these early stages of development, it is that people at ground zero are responding in four ways:

1. Providing services where gaps prevail as demonstrated in all three programs. Services take on different forms because the three programs have different missions. But even JUBILEE, which is more advocacy-minded, is helping congregations assess their capacity to deliver services, so that when they come to the public square they can, in fact say, what resources they can and cannot provide;

2. Providing community education. It is important for individuals and community institutions to learn about the magnitude of the problems created by policy changes, their direct affect on people, and also on institutions and community concerns that are indirectly involved;

3. Advocating for more coherent policies that Jubilee and the other programs are positioning themselves to develop at the state and community level. Because the program developers are "in the trenches," they are legitimate advocates for

fair policies. They are, in fact, at the initial stages of being the Community Samaritans, an idea discussed in the last chapter;

4. Demonstrating a concern for others. I have spent considerable time with each of the key people in these three programs. I am amazed at their concern for the plight of poor women and their children, the countless hours given on their behalf with little or no pay, and their sense that through their efforts, fairness and justice can preside to some extent in the lives of these women. I am sure that within the programs I have listed in the appendix to follow, the same spirit prevails. We need to learn as much as we can from those efforts.

APPENDIX

Innovative Practices: State-Wide Strategies

Below is a listing of programs around the country that I have come across that have some kind of partnership between public and religious organizations or some combination of public, nonprofit, and religious interconnection. They are in no particular order and when I have a contact person or phone number, I list it. Most of the information is taken with verbal permission from an article written by Jessica Yates (1998) called "Partnerships with the faith community in Welfare Reform," for the Welfare Information Network (www.welfareinfo.org) found on the Internet. What follows then is a list of articles reports and Internet addresses that outline the matters discussed here. Again, where there is the name or address of a contact person, I include it. Please remember that devolution has made it difficult to know what is happening and where. As noted above, options for involving the faith community in welfare reform range from informal collaborations to contracts for service provision. Examples from these state and local agencies, while not exhaustive, show the varying approaches to faith-government partnerships in welfare reform.

North Carolina. Mecklenburg County North Carolina: *A Faith Community United: The Faith Community/Department of Social Services Partner-*

ship Contact: Ralph Williamson Special Assistant to the Director, Religious Affairs 301 Billingsley Road, Charlotte, NC 28211, Phone 704–336–7512.

The Jobs Partnership of Raleigh. Working relationships and informal agreements between religious organizations providing services and local welfare caseworkers also can be fruitful. The Jobs Partnership of Raleigh in North Carolina is a nonprofit alliance of congregations and businesses. Individuals can participate in the 12-week program by their own volition or through referral from the local welfare agency. As the Jobs Partnership is assisting a client who is being considered for termination from welfare, often Partnership staff and volunteers are successful in requesting that the county welfare caseworker continue the client benefits while the individual is participating in the program. **Contact:** Skip Long, Director of the Jobs Partnership in Raleigh, at (919)571-8614, ext. 251, or see http://www.ccmangum.com/tjp.

Texas has stepped up efforts to involve the faith community and implement Section 104. A workgroup has formed to focus on ways to make the contracting process more accessible to all nonprofit organizations, and on noncontractual options for partnering with congregations and other nonprofits. These include informal collaborations, such as information-sharing to prevent duplicate services, or formal memoranda of understanding, such as client referral arrangements that define each organization role and responsibilities. Regional DHS offices have been asked to start reporting on a quarterly basis any new partnerships related to the implementation of Charitable Choice. **Contact:** Sharon Rowley, Texas DHS, (512) 438-4037.

Maryland's legislature defined specific opportunities for congregations and other nonprofits in welfare reform legislation in 1996 (SB 778) and 1997 (SB 499). The laws provided that nonprofit organizations can receive benefits on behalf of welfare recipients who are receiving up to three months of transitional assistance subsequent to being terminated from the regular welfare program. The 1996 law provided that a nonprofit acting as an intermediary for transitional assistance can use that funding to provide counseling, child care, housing, household supplies, and other non monetary aid to the welfare client. Faced with insufficient numbers of nonprofit organizations, in addition to implementing the basic thrust of Section 104 (Charitable Choice) of the welfare reform law (nondiscrimination for both religious organizations and welfare recipients), Maryland legislation includes other safeguards for recipients. SB 499 requires the Department of Human Resources to provide recipients with "clear and timely notice" of their rights under Section 104, such as the right to request an alternative provider. Contact Yolanda Parker, Office of Policy and Research, Department of Human Resources, (410) 767-7259.

In July 1994, the Anne Arundel County, Maryland, Department of Social Services began a pilot project offering welfare recipients the option of forgoing their direct cash welfare benefits and instead getting assistance passed through a community organization, which spends the money on behalf of the recipient. The pilot, called the Community-Directed Assistance Program (C-DAP), aimed to recruit all types of community nonprofits to act as sponsors. So far, all 27 of the sponsors have been congregations, which receive no monetary compensation. Participating organizations receive an up-front payment equal to six months of welfare benefits. The congregations are directed to work closely with the family for at least six months in providing supportive services, financial and job counseling, and related help. Congregations may not require that the family attend religious services. The county DSS provides technical assistance to the congregations throughout the process, and has started matching new sponsors with experienced congregations to promote the sharing of "best practices" and problem-solving techniques. In addition, potential referrals to C-DAP are now screened more thoroughly for criminal backgrounds and other "red flags." During the program the first three years, 33 families were referred to C-DAP, and 29 completed the program. **Contact** Christine Poulsen, Anne Arundel County DSS, at (410) 269-4460.

California. The San Diego County, California, Department of Social Services (DSS) created the All Congregations Together (ACT) initiative in 1996 as a way to involve congregations in the county response to community need. The first ACT team, which includes DSS, congregations and other nonprofit agencies, compiled a community resource manual for congregations, provided training regarding welfare reform, and established an ACT desk in the lobby of the local welfare office. The ACT desk, staffed by faith community volunteers, provides information to people in crisis and helps refer them to appropriate public and private resources. Some individuals and families may be diverted from welfare or general assistance, but ACT currently does not track this data. Congregations benefit by having a coordinated, efficient response to serving the needy, rather than individual congregations reacting each time a person contacts them for help. The congregations and the partnership have expressed interest in contracting opportunities as well. ACT is in the process of being incorporated as a 501(c)(3) nonprofit. **Contact:** Bobbie Neff, San Diego County DSS, at (619) 338-2014.

Virginia. Fauquier County, Virginia, was designated to be one of the first counties to implement the state welfare reform initiative in 1995. The county, in partnership with the local Virginia Cooperative Extension Unit and Department of Social Services, held a meeting for congregations and nonprofit organizations to obtain their input, and later conducted workshops for religious leaders to help them understand welfare reform and coordinate their response. These efforts helped stimulate the formation of an interfaith coalition that meets twice a month to continue assessing the community needs and to coordinate their resources. **Contact:** Beverly Butterfield, Virginia Extension Unit, at (540) 341-3950.

Michigan. As part of the Project Zero pilot, Ottawa County, Michigan contracted with Good Samaritan Ministries a religious nonprofit service provider in July 1996 to recruit, train and monitor congregations that "adopt" families on welfare. The contract was renewed in July 1997. Good Samaritan had already been facilitating adopt-a-family programs for the homeless on a smaller scale and without public funding. The county Family Independence Agency (FIA) then approached the organization about utilizing congregational resources for local welfare reform efforts as well. The FIA agency refers to Good Samaritan welfare clients who have their initial job placements, want to be mentored by a congregation, and do not have serious impediments to successful adopt-a-family participation. The agency's $100,000 contract with Good Samaritan lays out expectations on how families will be paired with congregations and how congregations will be trained. Good Samaritan then establishes a nonfinancial agreement with each congregation and family, which describes family goals, needs, strengths, and concerns, and includes a "plan of action" outlining what the ministry team and family will do to attain the goals. A congregation reports back to Good Samaritan on the family progress, which Good Samaritan reports back to the welfare agency. Congregations also make financial and in-kind donations to the Good Samaritan program. Approximately 150 out of 1,000 families in the county cumulative caseloads were referred the first year. **Contact:** Loren Snippe, Director of the Ottawa County FIA, (616) 394-

7200, and Goodwill Samaritan Ministries, at (616) 392-7159. Also see: http://www.mibusiness.com/ gsm/ and http://www.mfia.state.mi.us/projzero/projzero.htm

Ohio. Cuyahoga County, Ohio, recently awarded welfare contracts to two well-established, religiously affiliated service providers, the local Catholic Charities and the Jewish Family Services Association (JFSA). The welfare agency decision to contract with these organizations was based on their capacity, interest, ability, track record, and other typical criteria in human services contracting. Catholic Charities has a performance-based contract and receives its initial payment for placing a welfare recipient when he or she stays in the job for 30 days with the final payment received at attaining 90-day job retention. The county partnership with JFSA builds upon previous contracts for refugee resettlement programs. The contract is cost-reimbursement rather than performance-based, since JFSA is providing a wide range of services, not just job placement, under the contract. One question raised has been the extent to which a religiously affiliated organization can "market" its publicly funded services to populations of a particular faith. The county has restricted such targeting to avoid constitutional entanglements, but simultaneously recognizes that welfare contracts may affirm the strengths of organizations that provide culturally relevant and specific services that are needed. **Contact:** Joe Gauntner, Cuyahoga County Health and Nutrition, (216) 987-6640.

Nonspecific Partnerships

State and local agencies increasingly are establishing adopt-a-family and mentoring programs that are formal but nonfinancial arrangements. This approach builds on traditions within the faith community of assisting individuals and families through personal guidance and support. State welfare agencies and their local offices in Connecticut, Louisiana, Michigan, Mississippi, North Carolina, Texas, and Virginia are among those that have initiatives linking welfare families with congregations. These initiatives are voluntary for both congregations and welfare recipients, much like the Faith Matters initiative in Greensboro.

Typically, the welfare agency has the role of a technical assistance provider to the congregation and may request a written agreement outlining each party's responsibilities and goals. The congregation provides volunteer assistance that can include helping a welfare recipient budget his or her income, providing transportation to a job interview, aiding the recipient in finding child care and giving emotional support during difficult times. While most agencies tell participating congregations, they cannot insist that a welfare recipient attend their houses of worship, agencies generally do not place restrictions on other conversations pertaining to religion.

RESOURCE CONTACTS

Alliance for Redesigning Government, (202) 347-3190
http://www.alliance.napawash.org/alliance/index.html
American Jewish Congress, Marc Stern, (212) 879-4500,
   http://www.ajcongress.org
American Muslim Council, (202) 789-2262
Americans United for Separation of Church and State, Julie Segal,
   (202) 466-3234, http://www.au.org/leg-issu.htm
Call to Renewal, (202) 328-8842
Catholic Charities, (703) 549-1390, http://www.catholiccharitiesusa.org/
Center for Public Justice, Stanley Carlson-Thies, (410) 571-6300,
   http://www.cpjustice.org/cpjustice/
Center on Nonprofits and Philanthropy at the Urban Institute,
   Tobi Printz, (202) 828-1821, http://nccs.urban.org
Congress of National Black Churches, Sullivan Robinson, Interim
   Executive Director, (202) 371-1091, http://www.cnbc.org
Information Services Clearinghouse, Howard University Divinity School,
   (202) 806-0736
International Union of Gospel Missions, (816) 471-8020,
   http://www.iugm.org
Jim Castelli, Independent Writer/Researcher, (703) 250-3099,
   http://members.aol.com/jimcast/welcome.htm
Presbyterian Church (USA) Washington Office, The Rev. Elenora
   Giddings-Ivory, (202) 543-1126

PUBLICATIONS

"A Guide to Charitable Choice: The Rules of Section 104 of the 1996 Federal Welfare Law Governing State Cooperation with Faith-Based Social Service Providers," by the Center for Public Justice and the Christian Legal Society Center for Law and Religious Freedom, January 1997. (410) 571-6300 or see http://www.cpjustice.org/cpjustice/CGuide/Guide.html

"Arise, Take up Thy Mat, and Walk," by the Rev. Steven Burger, Policy Review: The Journal of American Citizenship, No. 79, Heritage Foundation, September–October 1996. (202) 546-4400 or see http://www.heritage.org/heritage/p_review/sept96/burger.html

"Church-Based Mentoring: A Program for Mentoring Ministries," United Way of Southeastern Pennsylvania, 1994. Contact the Points of Light Foundation, (800) 272-8306.

"Churches Help Make Welfare Reform Work," by Jay Hein, Hudson Institute Welfare Policy Center, 1997. (317) 549-4164 or see http://www.a1.com/hudson/wpc/articles/church.htm

"Constitutional and Policy Problems with Senator Ashcroft Charitable Choice Provisions," by Daniel E. Katz, ACLU, and Julie A. Segal, Americans United for Separation of Church and State, March 11, 1996. (202) 466-3234, http://www.aclu.org/congress/ashcrft.html

"Faith-Based Social Services: A Blessing, Not a Miracle," by Jim Castelli, for the Progressive Policy Institute, Policy Report No. 27, December 1997. (202) 547-0001 or see http://members.aol.com/jimcast/ppi.htm

"Guidelines for Constitutional Implementation of Welfare Reform by Religious Organizations," by the Working Group for Religious Freedom in Social Services, Americans United for the Separation of Church and State, 1998. (202) 466-3234 or see http://www.au.org/ash-imp.htm

"How to Think About Public Partnerships with Religious Organizations," by Jim Castelli, forthcoming, for the Alliance for Redesigning Government Public/Nonprofit High Performance Partnerships Program. (202) 347-3190.

"Implementation of Charitable Choice," Presbyterian Church (USA) Washington Office, 1998. Contact Douglas Grace at (202) 543-1126. 20

"Implementing Charitable Choice Provisions of Welfare Reform,"
Report of the Texas Department of Human Services Charitable
Choice Workgroup, May 1, 1997. (512) 438-4037 or see
http://www.dhs.texas.gov/regops/charitable/char1.htm

"New Hope for Gospel Missions? Devils in the Details," by the Rev.
Stephen Burger, International Union of Gospel Missions, Sept. 3, 1996.
(816) 471-8020 or see http://www.iugm.org/news/usatoday.html "Reli-
gion-Sponsored Social Service Providers: The Not-So-Independent Sector," by Jim Castelli and John D. McCarthy, for the Aspen Institute
Nonprofit Sector Research Fund, 1997. (410) 820-5236 or see
http://members.aol.com/jimcast/recent.htm#Aspen

"Services and Capacity of Religious Congregations in the Metropolitan
Area, Center on Nonprofits and Philanthropy, The Urban Institute,
1998. (202) 857-8687 or (202) 828-1821.

"Social and Community Involvement of Religious Congregations Housed
in Historic Religious Properties: Findings from a Six-City Study," Final
Report to Partners for Sacred Places, by Ram A. Cnaan, School of
Social Work, University of Pennsylvania, Dec. 2, 1997. (215) 898-5523.

"Wichita Medical Missionaries," by Steve Rabey, Policy Review: The
Journal of American Citizenship, No. 86, Heritage Foundation,
November–December 1997. (202) 546-4400 or see
http://www.policyreview.com/heritage/p_review/nov97/nation.html

Conclusion

Twenty-seven years ago I was young and socially concerned. I became a VISTA Volunteer because there was nothing more important to me than fighting the war on poverty. I was clearly an idealist. A major lesson I learned from that experience was that programs are implemented in the community, not at the drawing table at the statehouse or Washington. I quickly learned that there was a natural division between the distant politician, academic, or bureaucrat who theoretically knew how to fix a local problem and often set the wheels in motion for the fix without getting real input on how the locals might solve the same problem. The most valuable lesson that has turned me from being a true believer in any ideological position, is that I learned that even in the most rural communities, there is an indigenous system of services with its own identity, character, and culture. That system must be not be ignored when addressing social problems, changing social polices, or implementing new social programs. More often than not, the indigenous system gets ignored or taken for granted, and it is left to deliver something it cannot. And who gets the blame? The people who operate the system. The "ignoring and blaming" have been done by Democrats and Republicans alike.

Over the years, politicians of both political stripes have made convincing arguments why this or that policy is good or bad, why this or that program should be scrapped, and why this or that program should replace it. For those who do not work at the programmatic level, theoretical positions are often logical and airtight. For those who implement programs, the policy-making arena is vague, distant, controlling, and yet very influential and often harmful. During the last sixty-plus years of social service development, the question of how the programs get delivered locally has never been seen as a key factor that makes or breaks a policy. Much of policy development coming from the political right and the political left is stuck in their ideological positions. This book has been about the "rubber hitting the road." The rubber here is that the religious community can be a partner in service delivery, and that is all!

The gist of what I have said throughout this book comes down to this: as a society we would be better off focusing on building partnerships in the indigenous local systems of service so that the voluntary spirit that drives a good portion of the system can be nurtured. I spent time in the early chapters lightly elbowing the university. Academics would serve society well by increasingly testing how to solve some of our major problems. When we spend more time understanding how and why something works or doesn't work, we will be more effective in shaping the public discourse. Guiding the next era of service development through strong analysis will be helpful.

We will have to use the resources of the community to educate each other about the complex nature of the problems at hand, and how to solve, manage, or prevent those problems. The resources of the religious community are invaluable for education programs. If we can use the faith community's sacred space as community educational centers, we will be closer to carving out viable roles for all of the partners in the system of care. If we use these indigenous centers, some of the complex problems facing us will be understood by more and more people. If we could replace the myths and misconceptions that underscore much of our social policy debate, with the compassion and understanding, we will have a chance at building the partnerships in the local communities of care. If the forces of myths and misconceptions prevail, we will suffer.

Are there roadways that can be taken by the different drivers on that highway I described in chapter 7? I think so. For the purposes of framing the roles that different institutions might assume in the system of the new millennium, I'd like to use the example of a patchwork quilt to frame the discussion. A local system of services is made up of a complex series of patches that when connected care in somewhat effective ways for the people of the community. The agencies and organizations work from womb to tomb, helping the soon to be teen mom with prenatal care and the dying elderly person live the last stage of life with dignity through a hospice program. No single patch on a quilt, nor any combination of patches, when unstitched, can keep someone warm, and no uncoordinated, unplanned, and hostile service system can effectively solve, manage, or prevent a locality's problems. Governmental, educational, philanthropic, and religious institutions, each have a role to play in reshaping this system. Their roles are overlapping and interconnected.

Policymakers and planners would do well to initiate legislation that supports the development of local planning structures. I don't mean that they should merely put out a request for proposals for this project or that project and have a stage where a community could apply for a planning grant. We already have this system. I mean that we must move to a new way of conceptualizing relationships locally. As such, government, the largest partner in the scheme of delivery, must understand not only how it will change as roles and responsibilities change, but also that it must share that information with other partners in the system because their roles will inevitably change too. Failure to plan is a prescription for continual emergencies. Our system of services has been in emergency mode for almost two decades because we have made large policy shifts with little planning as to how the shifts would enhance or detract from effective delivery of services. Shrinking or adding to government program structures locally without planning how things should restitched as a result of the change is a formula for continued chaos.

City governments, for example, have departments of planning. There needs to be some configuration for the human-service partnerships to plan effectively at the local level. So if policymakers are so bent on making local systems the vehicles through which services get designed and delivered, then there has to be a planning arm to give accurate data upon which to make informed decisions and develop programs effectively. I believe that government is best equipped to provide the funds for the development of such structures and I think that local educational institutions would be a strong candidates, but not necessarily the only ones, to assume the research, policy, and evaluation functions on a systematic basis. Some might say we have that system already within the child welfare, mental health, and elder care systems, but I would argue that at best these are fragile links in a fragmented system of federal and state support to higher education via "social service research and training." We need desperately to strengthen the research, development, and planning functions within the large and complicated local systems of service. The more myth and rumor that underscores local service development, the more rhetoric, and vitriol that will lace the actual delivery of services.

The educational community can assume the role it plays best in the new local system and that is the role of "educator." I envision every community having a research and development arm in one, or a consortium of local institutions that serve as the human services equivalent of the research and development arm of a company like Intel. I would expect that over the long run such a mechanism would save billions of dollars in wasteful spending because the system would not solve its problems through rhetoric and guesswork, but through systematic research and evaluation. We could actually tell with a degree of more accuracy than we now have, whether some policy notion would actually work in a particular area, because the idea was based on an accurate assessment of available resources. The research about the idea's feasibility was conducted by an institution with the ability to provide accurate data and respected interpretation. Over the period of fifty to seventy-five years, the providers in local systems would begin to think and do things differently.

That is but one piece of the puzzle. Educational institutions must reconceptualize their curricula, especially in the fields with applied components like Social Work, Human Development, Housing and Urban Design, Nursing, Education, Theology, Public Administration, Nonprofit Management, Public Health, Recreation Management, Criminal Justice and others along those lines. On Main Street, many of the people trained in such fields work with each other regularly, and sometimes at cross purposes or even with hostility. The disciplinary lenses through which they learned to see the world during their academic training sometimes makes them unnecessarily myopic. A wider scope is need for good collaboration on Main Street. I would base the curricula in the traditional knowledge base of a particular field with a clear understanding that the field of practice is centering increasingly around the interplay of politics, social service, and religion. I believe that the classroom curriculum ought to be based partly in political economy (this covers a broad range of areas from history of nonprofits to social problems and community studies) and partly in applied program planning and development (which also covers a broad range of areas from strategic planning to grant writing and program evaluation). I would also consider extending the course work so that it covers the material necessary to put skilled practitioners into the field.

I noted the growth of Greensboro Urban Ministry in an earlier chapter. On closer inspection of the figure, it is easy to see the variety of the populations, systems, and institutions that operate just in this one program of Greensboro Urban Ministry. For example, there are homeless individuals, homeless families, the working poor, two faith-based organizations working in collaboration with each other, the church-based volunteers, the business community, federal, and state agencies and local government. Some might think that one who is employed in a faith-based nonprofit organization can learn on the job. I wouldn't mind members of my volunteer corps learning on the job. I would, however, like to hire new staff that have the knowledge, skills, and ability to work skillfully and successfully with the people and institutions—which range from the homeless family to the foundation officer—from the get go. Institutions of higher education will have to make some adjustments to their curricula if they are going to succeed at meeting this new demand.

Consequently, in the applied area of the curriculum, an interdisciplinary focus would be extremely helpful for future practitioners to work most effectively in the interdisciplinary world where they practice. Divinity students for example, would do well to know what case management (in figure 10.1 above) is before they have to apply for a grant asking for a case manager. Believe it or not, there is an extensive literature on case management. Grant writing is also something they, and other students, could learn before they actually have to spend hours on the job learning that art and craft. There is an extensive literature on this subject as well. Social work and public administration students ought to know something about the workings of congregations, denominations, and faith-based nonprofit organizations. Increasingly, internships should be crafted collaboratively across disciplines, and coordinated so that interns from different disciplines start their internships together and learn about each other in the practice setting.

Greensboro Urban Ministry has divinity student interns, but no social work student interns. They could each benefit from each other's training.

It would take a while to redo curricula so I would address some of the most pressing academic needs with course modules. I won't go into detail about them. Rather I will just note them. They include short courses which might cover Budgeting, Case Management, Faith and Service, Understanding and Negotiating the Community System, Church and Government Relations, Partnering with other Faith Traditions, Program Planning, Grant Writing and Fund Raising, Working with the Media, Volunteer Management, Developing a Nonprofit Corporation, Board Development, Needs Assessment, Program Evaluation and Technological Development. I am sure there are numerous others.

The private philanthropic community, could better serve as stewards by enticing educational institutions toward more integrative approaches by offering grants that have collaborative aspects to them. The Bonner Foundation's Bonner's Scholar Program is a model that could be built upon. It affords low-income students scholarships to do internships in nonprofit agencies. This kind of assistance could be extended to faculty/nonprofit collaborations in interdisciplinary curriculum development, and collaborative interdisciplinary internships within and across educational institutions in local communities. The more minds working together, the better chance we have of success.

There has been much said in the philanthropic community about capacity building in the last decade, but this has usually been from the perspective of building this or that organization's capacity to deliver services effectively. I have argued throughout this book that policies that don't take into account the intricate links in the local partnership of services are doomed. The same principle holds true for organizations. If they try to strengthen their capacity to deliver services with a limited focus on their connections with the local system of services, they too will be far less successful than they anticipated. The philanthropic community would go far in providing assistance in linking systems and organizations in the community, thus providing the necessary foundation upon which nonprofit organizations can build their true capacity to function effectively. I noted a couple of ideas in the preceding paragraph. Foundations, as part of an evaluation, could also require that agencies keep data in manageable forms, and support that requirement with funds. The data might include information about linkages with other organizations especially congregations. The larger governmental/educational planning operations I noted above, will need agencies to be able to supply accurate information before any systemic analysis can take shape with any degree of accuracy. The current incremental approach to funding this or that project sustains the organization's ability to meet payroll, but not necessarily its ability to serve any more effectively. Eventually, the system will need to have some kind of coherence, and that will take planning and funding. The philanthropic community will need to step to the plate.

In order for communities to solve, manage, and prevent the range of their problems effectively there needs to be a wider understanding of the problems they face. As I noted in chapter 8, eventually the congregations that provide the resources will shape the moral tone of the community. One of the important lessons I learned from one of my case studies of how agencies bring congregations into their sphere of resources is that the process is developmental. Congregations that might be considered outside of the loop on a particular controversial issue like AIDS for example, are sometimes approachable if the discussion is about AIDS babies. The particular example from I am drawing here was with regard to a presentation that the then director of the agency that serves people with HIV made at a conservative church. While the church was unwilling to make an institutional commitment of finances or volunteers, the director did receive several letters from parishioners who heard the presentation and were willing to help as citizens and not representatives of their church. If the community is to be successful in service delivery, it will have to be educated. Congregations are natural places for that education because, as I have demonstrated, they deliver a broad range of services, and assist community agencies likewise.

As we move deeper into this next stage of development it might be appropriate to consider the deeper implications of the lesson learned from the HIV example. Citizens are congregants and congregants are citizens. Community institutions shape the environment but people shape their institutions as well. It is plausible that a couple of the people from the congregation I just mentioned do volunteer as citizens and learn a great deal about AIDS babies. They come back to their parishes and slowly but surely discuss the issue in their adult Sunday school classes. A deeper understanding of the complexities follows, and the Sunday school class decides to "adopt" an AIDS baby for Christmas—providing it with gifts. Not only does the child benefit in this scenario, but the institution begins the process, slowly, to enter as a Public Samaritan into the partnership. Agencies and congregations would do well to envision themselves as partners in educating the citizenry about the range of problems and range of roles the citizens might play in ameliorating them. When the collective educational and service efforts of a community's congregations are underscored with education, a foundation can be laid to understand the meaning of the data that hopefully will be collected on a systematic basis. Only then will the congregations involved in service provision have the basis to provide moral leadership on solving local problems.

We will need the interplay of government stimulating educational planning, the philanthropic community working with the education, religious, and nonprofit community, and all working hard to educate each other to successfully manage our complex social problems.

As Professor Roy Lubove always reminded his students (and I was one of them) in his often blunt way: "social policy is complex despite the simple mindedness of its formulators." Let us all work hard to make better communities through thoughtful and carefully researched debate, discussion, and program development. The devil in devolution is in the details of program planning and development.

REFERENCES

Associated Press. 1996. Clinton asks churches to hire welfare receivers, *Greensboro News and Record* (September 7), A2.

Associated Press. 1996. DSS Head: Churches Can Help Reform Welfare. *Greensboro News and Record* (October 22), B2.

Axinn June, and Herman Levin. 1982. *Social Welfare: A History of the American Response to Need*. 2nd ed. New York: Harper and Row.

Begbie, Harold. 1920. *The Life of General William Booth*. New York: Macmillan.

Berger, P. and R. Neuhaus. 1977. *To Empower People*. Washington, D.C.: American Enterprise Institute for Public Policy Research.

Bernick, E. Lee and David Pratto. 1991. *The Voters Perspective: A Report to the Commissioners of Guilford County*. April 15. University of North Carolina at Greensboro.

Birnbaum, Jeffery, H. 1995. The Right Hand Of God. *Time* (June 15): 29–35.

Bremner, R. H. 1972 [1960]. *From the Depths: The Discovery of Poverty in the United States*. 6th ed. New York: NYU Press.

Carlton-Thies, Stanley, W., and James W. Skillen, eds. 1996. *Welfare in America: Christian Perspectives on a Policy in Crisis*. Grand Rapids, MI: William B. Erdmans Publishing Company.

Cassety, Judith H., and Ruth Mcroy. 1983. "Gender Race and the Shrinking Welfare Dollar, Women with Children Especially Blacks Are in Jeopardy. *Public Welfare* (Summer): 36–39.

Catholic Charities USA. 1998. ADVOFAX, March, 18

Center For Public Justice, The Center for Law and Religious Freedom. 1997. *A Guide to Charitable Choice: The Rules of Section 104 of the 1996 Federal Welfare Law Governing StateCooperation with Faith Based Social Service Providers*. Washington DC and Annandale Virginia

Chavez, Tim. 1995. "We Must Finally Give a Damn." *Utica Observer Dispatch* July 9.

Claman, V.N., and D. E. Butler, with J. A. Boyatt. 1994. *Acting On Your Faith: Congregations Making a Difference: A Guide to Success in Service and Social Action*. Boston, Insights.

Cnaan, R.A. 1997. "Social and Community Involvement of Religious Congregations Housed in Historic Religious Properties—A final Report to Partners for Sacred Places." Philadelphia.

Cnann, R.A. with Robert J. Wineburg and Stephanie Boddie. 1999. *The Newder Deal: Social Work and Religion in Partnership*. New York: Columbia University Press.

Coll, Blanch. 1973. *Perspectives in Public Welfare*. Washington, D.C.: Department of Health Education and Welfare.

Congressional Budget Office of The Congress of The United States. 1983. Major Legislative Changes in Human Resources Programs since January 1981. Staff Memorandum, August.

Demko, Paul, Faith Based Charites to the Rescue? 1997. *Chronicle of Philanthropy* 10(5): 12/11.

Denton, Herbert, H. 1982. "Reagan Urges More Church Aid for Needy." *Washington Post* A3. April, 14.

De Schweinitz, Karl. 1975. *England's Road to Social Security*. New York: A. S. Barnes.

Dobkin Hall, P. 1990. "The History of Religious Philanthropy in America." In R. Winthrow and V. Hodgkinson, eds. *Faith and Philanthropy in America*. San Francisco: Josey-Bass.

Doll, William. 1984. Cooperation in Cleveland. *Foundation News* 5: 66–70.

Edwards, B. 1995. "Mississippi Families Asked to Adopt Welfare Families, Morning Edition, National Public Radio Transcript #1579–8, April 6.

Faith Matters Documents. 1998, February and April 1.

Federal Register, March 8, 1990. p. 8555

Fitzgerald, Kevin. 1998. Letter To Marvin Pittman Lincoln County Department of Social Srvice pp. 1–5. North Carolina Department of Human Resources, February 27.

Fox-Piven, Francis, and Richard Cloward. 1983. "Toward a Class Based Realignment of American Politics." *Social Policy* 3 (Winter): 3–14.

Frame, Randy. 1995. "Religious Nonprofits Fight for Government Funds." *Christian Century* 39(14): 65.

French M. A. 1991. "At nw church Dixon Urges Concern for the Poor." *The Washington Post* (September 23), A7.

The George Gilder Home Page. 1998. Vintage George Gilder: George Gilder as Interviewed in *Playboy* Magazine in 1981. Http://www.Discovery.org/Gilder/ggPlayboy.HTML

Greensboro News and Record. 1991. "Passing The Buck" (September 1), A1.

Greensboro News and Record. 1996. Section A4, July 25. (No title: Governor Hunt Article).

Harriston Otis. 1991. *Greensboro News and Record* (April 13) Letter To the Editor.

Hershberg, Theodore. 1989. "Universities Must Devote More Time and Money to Policy Research at the State and Local Levels." *The Chronicle Of Higher Education* (November 8): B1–2.

Hodgkinson, Virginia, Murray Weitzman, and A. Kirsh. 1988. *From Belief To Commitment: The Activities and Finances of Religious Congregations in the United States: Findings from A National Survey.* Washington, DC. Independent Sector.

Hodgkinson, V. M. Weitzman, A. Kirsh, A. Noga, and H. Gorski. 1993. *From Belief To Commitment: The Activities and Finances of Religious Congregations in the United States: Findings from A National Survey.* Washington, DC. Independent Sector.

Johnson, F. E., ed. 1956. *Religion and Social Work.* New York: Institute for Religious and Social Studies.

Jubilee Document. 1997. No Date.

Kammer, Fred, SJ. 1997. Government Has a Responsibility to Poor Families. *Non Profit Times*, July, p. 50.

Klein, Joe. 1997, "In God They Trust." *The New Yorker* 73 (16): 40–48.

Linder, E. W., M. C. Mattis, and J.R. Rogers. 1983. *When Churches Mind The Children: A Study of Day Care in Local Parishes.* Ypsilanti, MI: The High Scope Press.

Lubove, Roy. 1965.*The Professional Altrusits: The Emergence of Social Work as a Career.* New York: Atheneum.

Lubove, Roy. 1992. Personal Converation, September 23.

Magill, R.S. 1986. "Social Welfare Politics in Urban America." *Social Work* 31 (5).

Maguire, G. H. 1985. "A Course to Train Church Volunteers to Interact with the Aged, Ill and Handicapped." *Physical and Occupational Therapy in Geriatrics* 4 (1): 45–51.

Marty, Martin. 1980. "Godly and godless." *Social Service Review* (December): 463–481.

McDonald, Jean A. 1984. "Survey Finds Religious Groups Strongly Favor More Collaboration." *Foundation News* (September–October): 20–24.

McDonald, Mark. 1984. Food Recipients: New Distribution Much Improved. *Greensboro News and Record*, C1. August 23.

Mead, Lawrence, M.(1986) *Beyond Entitlement: The Social Obligations of Citizenship.* New York: The Free Press.

Mitchell, C. 1990. "Memphis Group Drafts Biblical Strategy to Help the Poor." *Atlanta Journal And Constitution* (April 4), A 4.

Moberg, David, O. 1962. *The Church as a Social Institution.* Englewood Cliffs, N.J., Prentice-Hall.

Monsma, Stephen. 1996. *When Sacred and Secular Mix.* Lanham, MD.: Rowman & Littlefield.

Mullen, Betty. 1982. *Community Research External Appraisal* Junior League of Greensboro, February 17.

Murray Charles. 1984 [1983]. *Losing Ground America Social Policy 1950–1980* Tenth Anniversary Edition. New York: Basic Books.

Nathan, Richard P., Frederick C. Doolittle, et al. 1983. *The Consequences of Cuts: The Effects of the Reagan Domestic Program on State and Local Governments.* Princeton, N.J.: Princeton Urban and Regional Research Center. Distributed by Princeton University Press.

Nathan, Richard P., Frederick C. Doolittle, et al. 1987 *Reagan and the States.* Princeton: Princeton University Press.

Negstad, J. and R. Arnholt, R. 1986. "Day Centers for Older Adults: Parish and Agency Partnership. *Journal of Religion and Aging* 4: 25–33.

Netting, F. Ellen. 1982. "Church-related Agencies and Social Welfare." *Social Services Review* 58(3): 404–420.

Netting F. Ellen. 1984. "The Changing Environment: Its Effects on Church Related Agencies. *Social Services Review* 2(1): 16–30.

North Carolina Budget and Tax Center Report (August 1996) 2 (17): 3.

Olasky, Marvin. 1992. *The Tragedy of American Compassion.* Washington, D.C.: Regnery.

Orr, J. B., D. E. Miller, W. E. Roof, and J. G. Melton. 1994. *Politics of the Spirit: Religion and Multi-ethnicity in Los Angeles.* (A preliminary report of research conducted under the auspices of The Religion and Civic Order Project at UC Santa Barbara and the University of California, Los Angeles, and The University of Southern California.

Peeler, Alexandra. 1985. *Parish Social Ministry: A Vision and Resource: A Catholic Perspective.* Washington, D.C.: National Conference of Catholic Charities.

Rainbow Research. 1991. *Religious Institutions as Partners in Community Based Development:* Findings from Year One Of the Lilly Endowment Program. Minneapolis: Rainbow Research.

The Reagan Home Page (1997, August version) *Reagan's Speech to the Annual Prayer Breakfast* [WWW document] http://pages.prodigy.com/christianhmsc/speech1.htm

The Reagan Home Page (1997, August version) "A Time For Choosing, a.k.a. The speech." [WWW document] http://www.empower.org.townhall/hall_of_fame/reagan/sppeech/the_spee.htm.

Reid, William J. and Peter K. Stoimson. 1987. "Sectarian Agencies." *Encyclopedia of Social Work* 2: 545–54.

Roozen, D. A., W. McKinney, and J. Carroll. 1984. *Varieties of Religious Presence: Mission in Public Life.* New York: Pilgrim Press.

Rosenberry, Sara, A. 1983. "National Welfare Commitments Under the Reagan Administration." *Journal of Urban Affairs* (Winter): 10–20.

Salamon, Lester. 1992. *America's Nonprofit Sector.* New York: The Foundation Center.

Salamon, Lester M. and Fred Teitelbaum. 1984. "Religious Congregations as Social Service Agencies: How Extensive Are They? *Foundation News* (September–October): 62–65.

Salamon, Lester M., D. M. Altschuler, and C. J. DeVita. 1985. *Chicago Nonprofit Organizations: The Challenge of Retrenchment.* Urban Institute Research Report. Washington, D.C.

Salamon, Lester M., D. M. Altschuler, and J. Myllyluomo. 1990 *More Than Just Charity: The Baltimore Nonprofit Sector in a Time of Change.* Baltimore: The Johns Hopkins Institute For Policy Studies.

Selinske, Joanne, F. 1983. "Protecting CPS Clients and Workers: Guidelines Can Help Workers." *Public Welfare* (Summer): 31–35.

Shapiro, J. P. 1996. "The Faith Factor: Can Churches Cure America's Social Ills?" *US News and World Report* 121 (10): 46–54.

Sherman, A. L. 1995. "Cross Purposes: Will Conservative Welfare Reform Corrupt Religious Charities? *Policy Review* no. 74. URL File////A/thser.html.

Sherman, A. L. 1997a. An evaluation of Mississippi's faith and families initiative: A report prepared for the workshop on Implementing Government Cooperation with Religious Social Ministries. Washington, DC and Annandale, Virginia: Center For Public Justice and The Center for Law and Religious Freedom.

Sherman, A. L. 1997b. Fruitful collaboration between religious groups and governmental entities: Lessons from Virginia and Maryland. A report prepared for the workshop on Implementing Government Cooperation with Religious Social Ministries. Washington, DC and Annandale, Virginia: Center For Public Justice and The Center for Law and Religious Freedom.

Shotzberger M. 1996. "The Government Taketh, but It Also Provides Us Needed Services." *Greensboro News and Record.* June 2, F3.

Shuman, Michael H. 1998. Why do Progressive Foundations Give Too Little To Too Many? *The Nation* 266 (2): 11–15.

Trost, C.,(1988). "Debate Over Day Care Bill Spurs Odd Alliances Raises Issues of Church State Separation." *The Wall Street Journal* (August 29): 32.

Tumulty, Karen. 1999. "Taking a Leap of Faith." *Time* 152 (22) (June 7).

United Way of America. 1994. Setting the strategic direction for the United Way System: Discussion draft.

United Way of America. 1996. Director of Research—Linda Nadich, July 14.

Weintraub, D. M. 1992. "Clerics Meet Wilson, Oppose Welfare Cuts. *Los Angeles Times* (March 26), A 27.

Welfare Reform Liaison Project Planning Document. November, 1997.

Wendt Oliver, and Patrick Adamacik. 1982. "A Letter To President Reagan." *Charities USA* 9 (7) September.

Wilensky, Harold. L., and Charles Lebeaux. 1958. *Industrial Society and Social Welfare: The Impact of Industrialization on the Supply and Organization of Social Welfare in the United States.* New York: Russell Sage Foundation.

Willis, Garry. 1990. *Under God: Religion and American Politics,* New York: Simon and Schuster.

Wineburg, C. R. and R. J. Wineburg. 1987. "Local Human Service Development: Institutional Utilization of Volunteers to Solve Community Problems." *Journal of Volunteer Administration* 5 (4): 9–14.

Wineburg, R. 1984. The Future of Human Services: Pulling Together or Tearing Apart. *Public Welfare* 3: 26–31.

Wineburg, R. J. 1996a. "An Investigation of Religious Support of Public and Private Agencies in One Community in an Era of Retrenchment." *Journal of Community Practice* 3 (2): 35–56.

Wineburg, R. J. 1996b. "Relationships Between Religion and Social Services: An Arranged Marriage or Renewal of Vows?" *Social Work and Christianity* 23 (1): 9–27.

Wineburg, R. J. and C. R. Wineburg. 1986. "Localization of Human Services: Using Church Volunteers to Fight the Feminization of Poverty." *Journal of Volunteer Administration* 4(3): 1–6.

Wineburg, R. J. and C. R. Wineburg. 1987 "Local Human Service Development: Institutional Utilization of Volunteers to Solve Community Problems." *Journal of Volunteer Administration* 4(1):9–14.

Wineburg, R. J., F. Ahmed, and M. Sills. 1997. "Local Human Service Organizations and the Local Religious Community During an Era of Change. *Journal of Applied Social Sciences* 21 (2): 93–98.

Wineburg, R., P. Spakes, and J. Finn. 1983. "Budget Cuts and Human Services: One Community's Experience. *Social Casework* 64(8): 489–96.

Wineburg, Samuel S. 1987. The Self Fulfillment of the Self Fulfilling Prophecy: A Critical Appraisal. *Educational Researcher,* 16 (9). (December): 28–44.

Wisner, Stan. 1983. "Fighting Back: A Critical Analysis of Coalition Building in the Human Services." *Social Services Review* 2 (June): 291–305.

Yates, Jessica. 1998. Partnerships With the Faith Community In Welfare Reform (Internet Document (*www.welfareinfo.org*) By Permission April, 22 1998.

INDEX

Locators for figures are in *italic*. Locators for tables are followed by *t*.